HISTORY OF THE GREAT WAR

GALLIPOLI

ATLAS

HISTORY OF THE GREAT WAR

BASED ON OFFICIAL DOCUMENTS
BY DIRECTION OF THE HISTORICAL SECTION
COMMITTEE OF IMPERIAL DEFENCE

MILITARY OPERATIONS

GALLIPOLI

ATLAS

MAPS AND SKETCHES COMPILED BY

MAJOR A. F. BECKE

R.A. (RETIRED), HON. M.A. (OXON.)

VOL. I

INCEPTION OF THE CAMPAIGN
TO MAY 1915

The Naval & Military Press Ltd

Published by

The Naval & Military Press Ltd
Unit 5 Riverside, Brambleside
Bellbrook Industrial Estate
Uckfield, East Sussex
TN22 1QQ England

Tel: +44 (0)1825 749494

www.naval-military-press.com
www.nmarchive.com

In reprinting in facsimile from the original, any imperfections are inevitably reproduced and the quality may fall short of modern type and cartographic standards.

SKETCHES

[*N.B.*—The spelling of the place-names in the Sketches and Maps agrees with the rulings, where such have been given, of the Royal Geographical Society's Permanent Committee on Geographical Names.]

1. The Theatre of Operations
2. Germany's Eastern Ambition, 1914
3. Constantinople and the Bosporus
4. The Objectives for 25th April
5. Turkish Dispositions before the Landings
5A. Dispositions of the Turkish 9th Division, Dawn, 25th April
6. The Three Anzac Ridges
7. Anzac
8. Y Beach
8A. The Helles Beaches on 25th April
9. V Beach 9 A.M., 25th April
10. Kum Kale and Yeni Shehr
11. The Landings. Situation at Dusk, 25th April
12. Gully Ravine (from British Map)
13. Gully Ravine (from Turkish Map)
14. First Battle of Krithia
15. Anzac. Approximate British Front Line, end of April
16. Attack on Baby 700, 2nd May
17. Turkish Night Attack, 1st/2nd May
18. Objectives for the Second Battle of Krithia
19. The Second Battle of Krithia, 6th–8th May

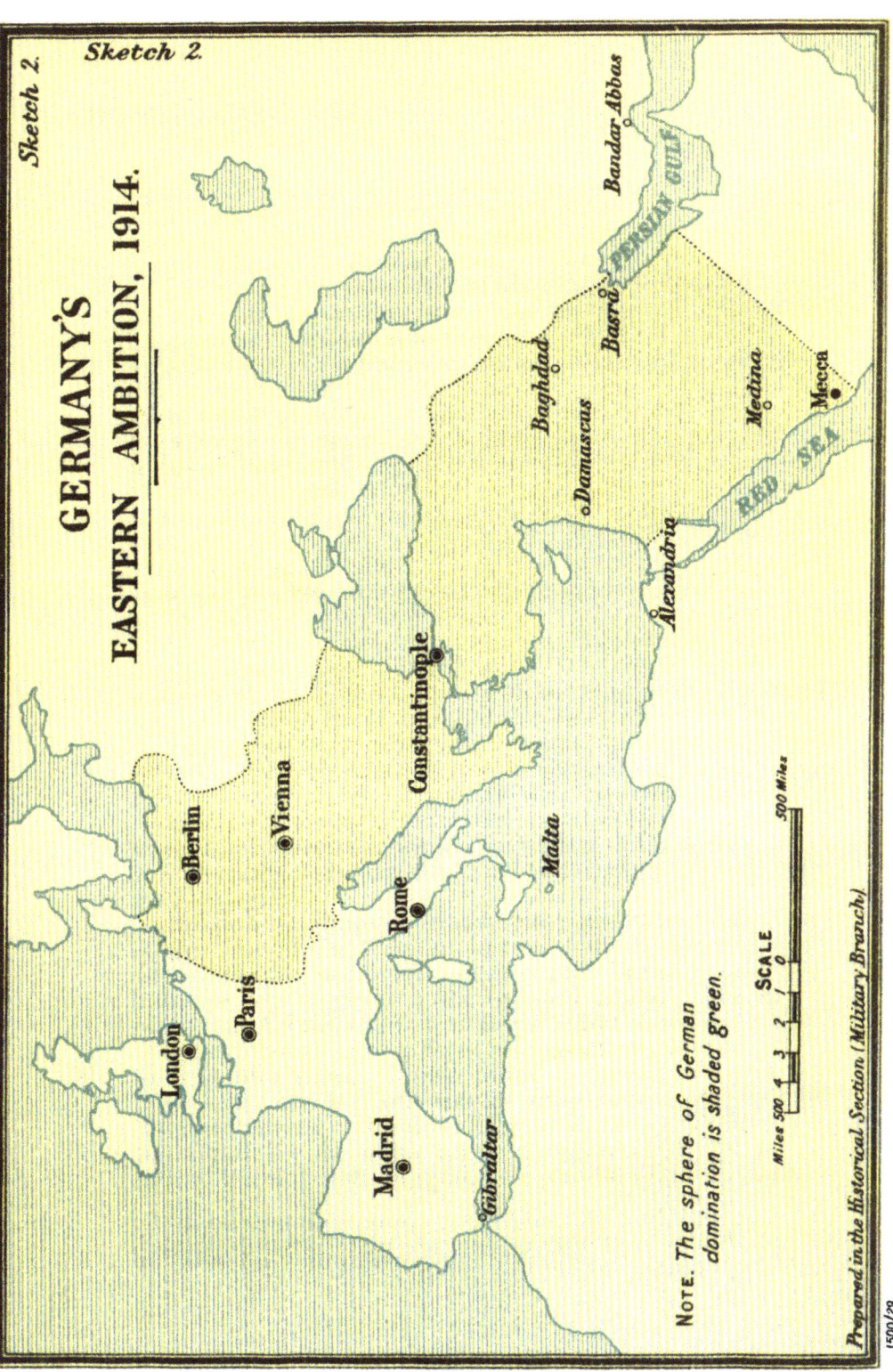

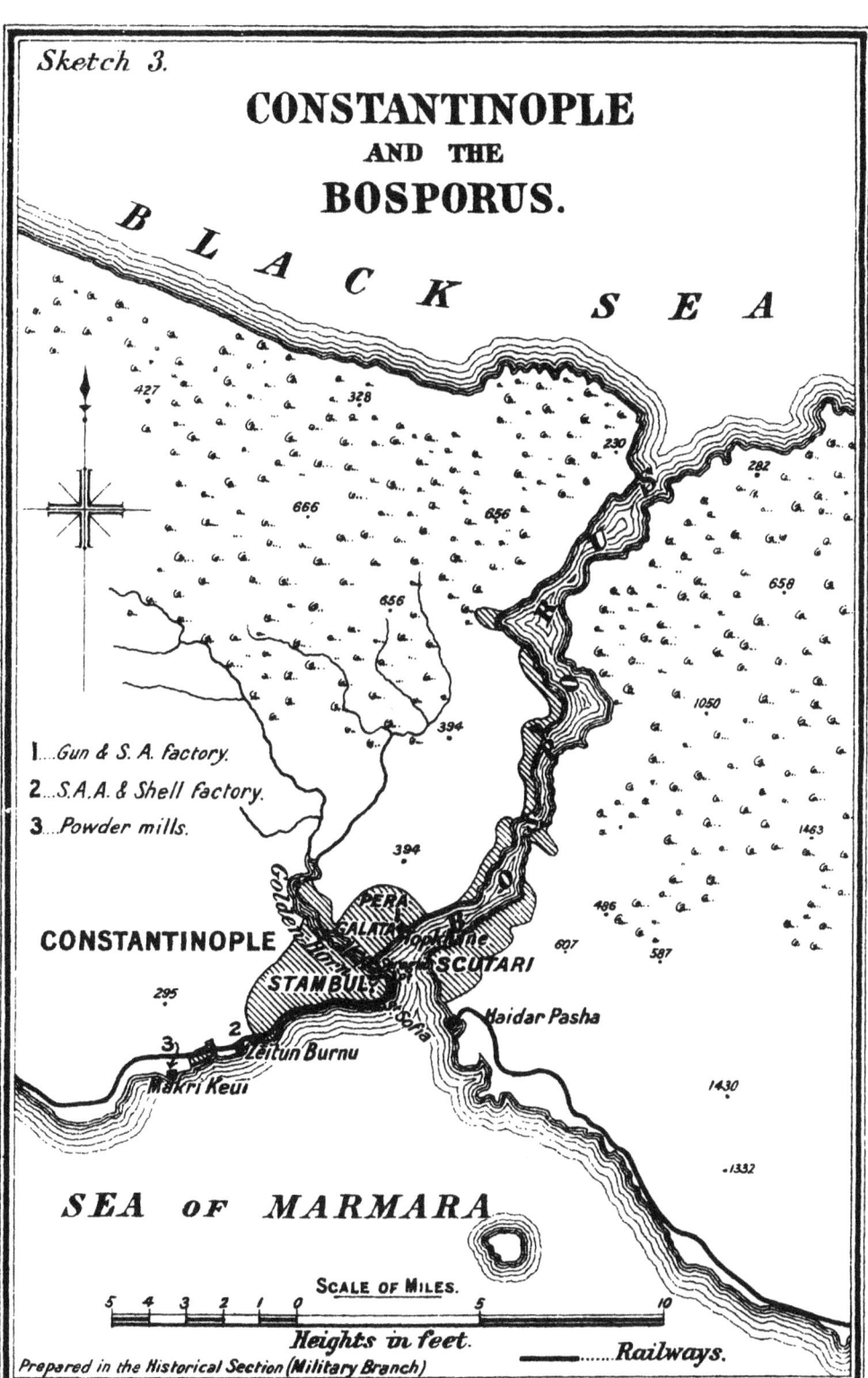

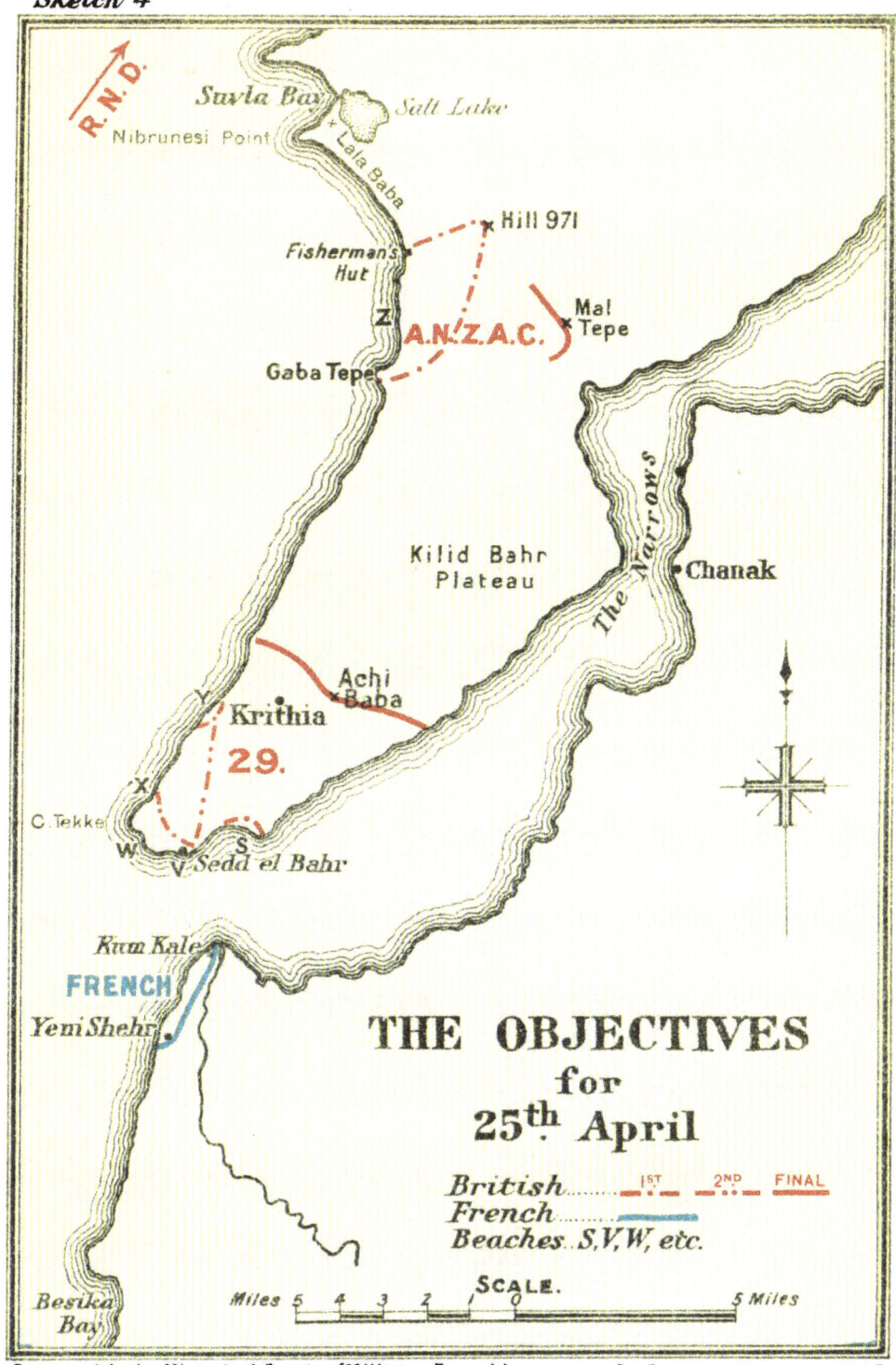

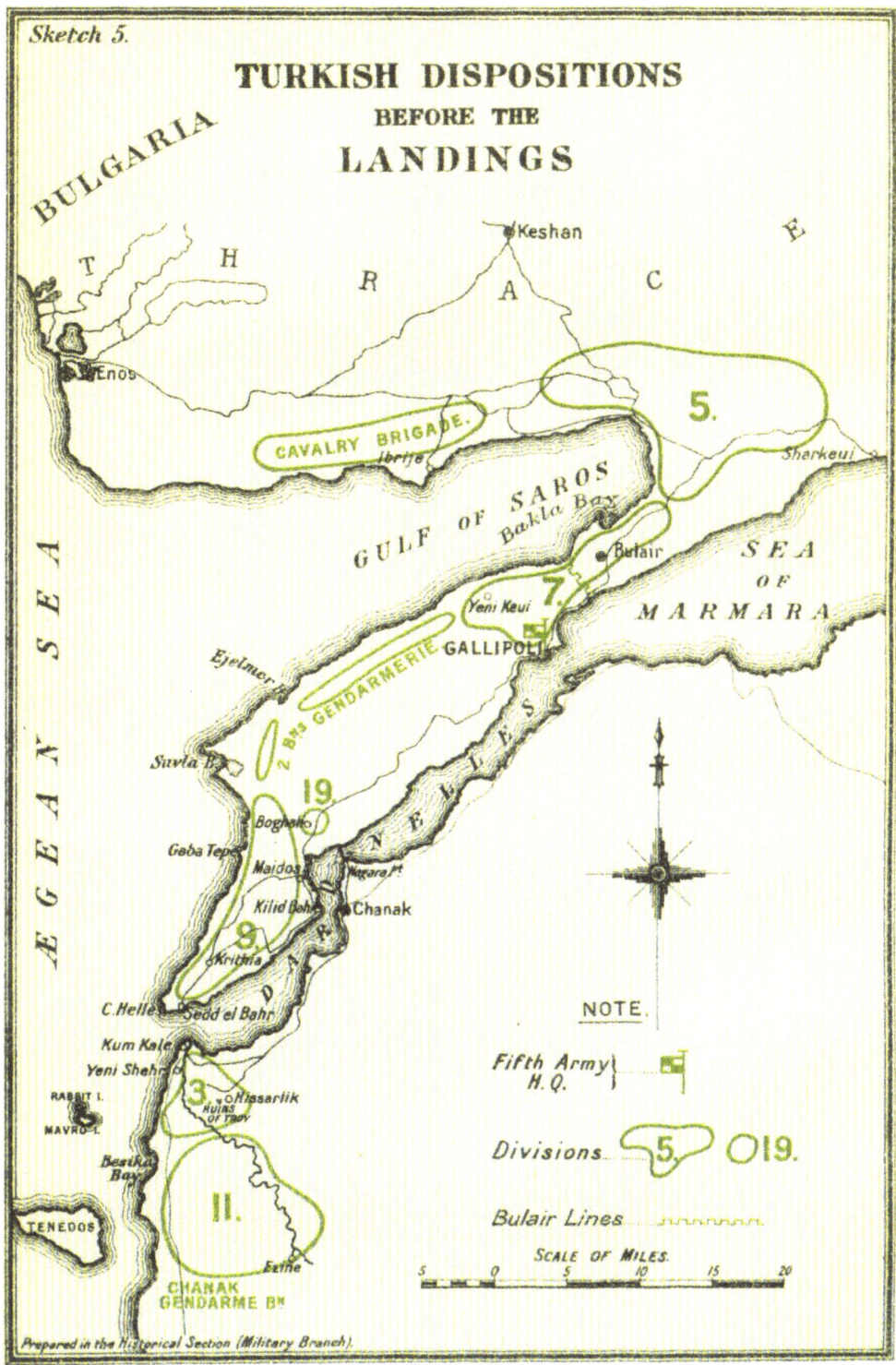

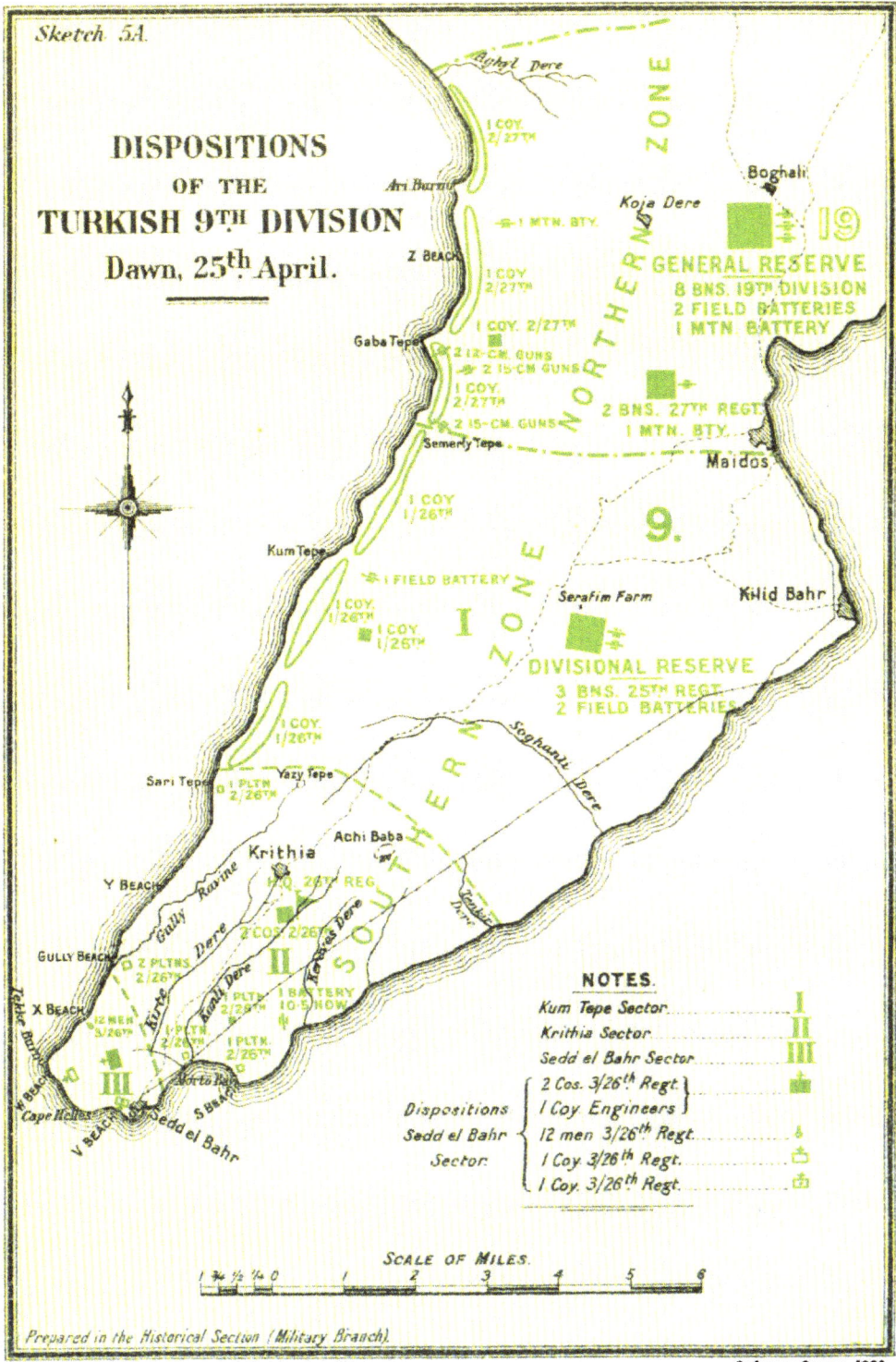

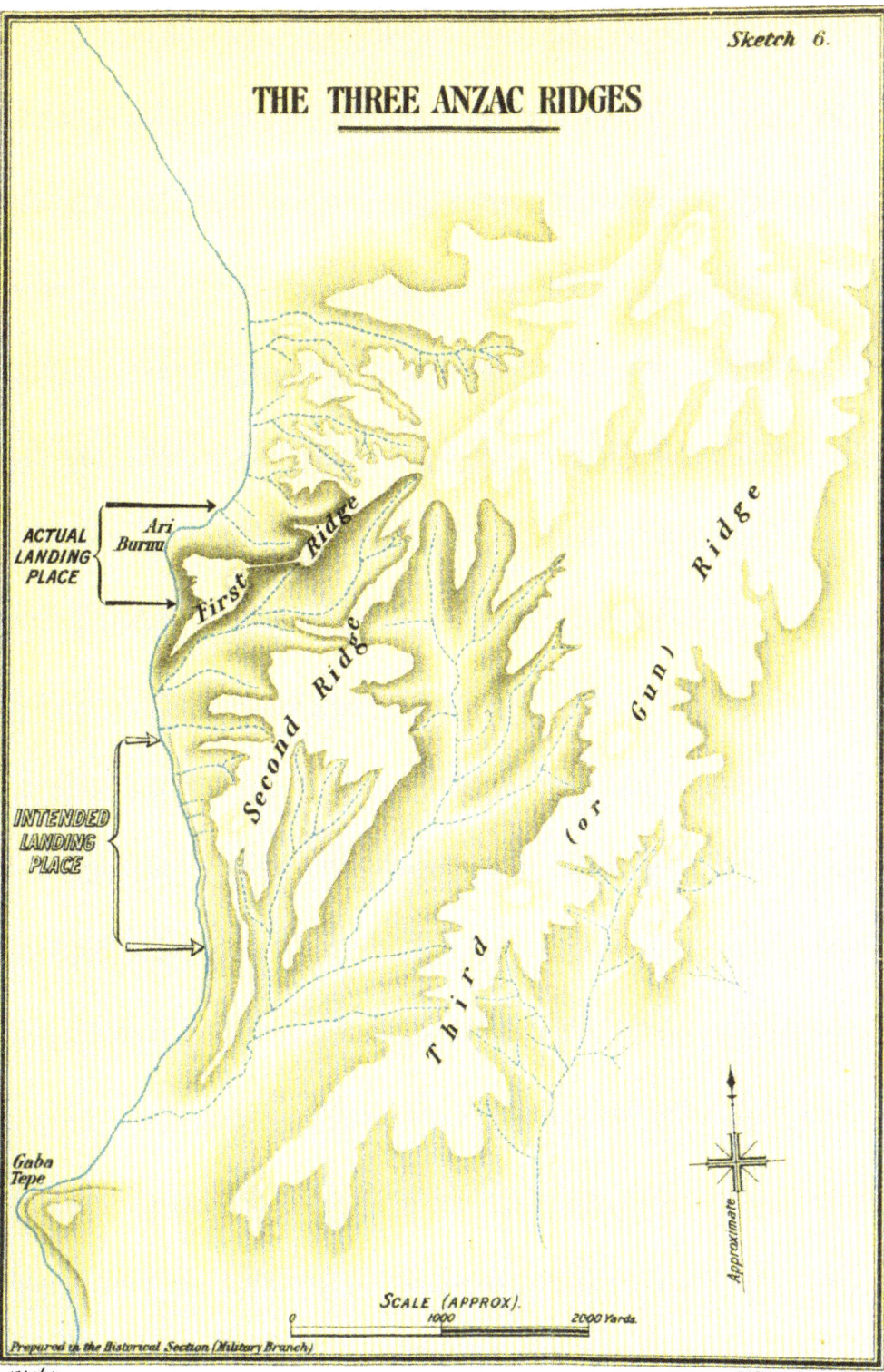

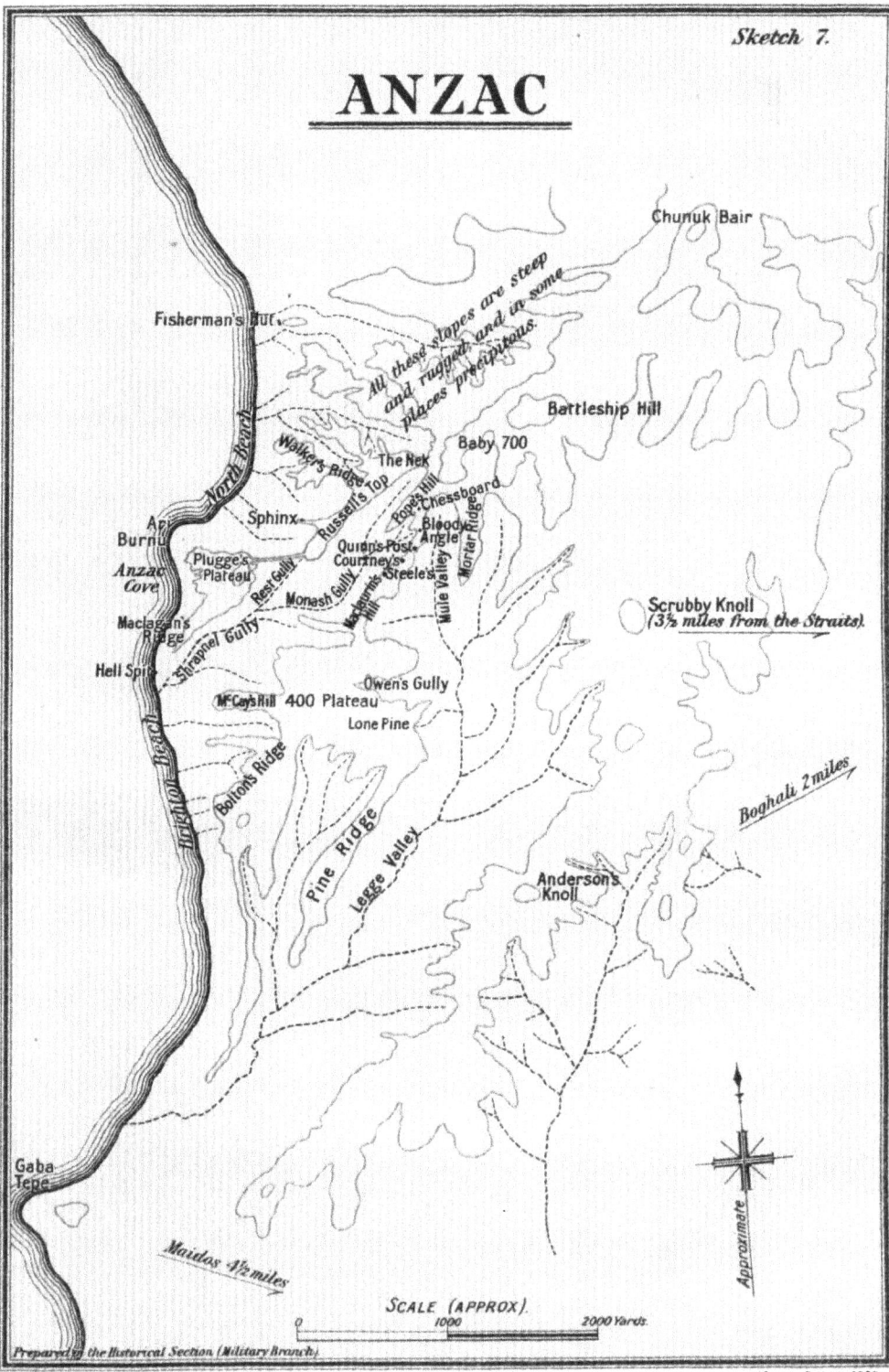

Sketch 8.

Y BEACH
(Reduced from the Turkish 1:5000 Survey)

Attack by 1st 25th Reg't

Krithia

Achi Baba 1 mile

Y BEACH

Gully Ravine

SCALE
Heights in feet.

Prepared in the Historical Section (Military Branch).

Ordnance Survey, 1928

Sketch 8.

HELLES
The Beaches & the Turkish Defences
25th April 1915.

REFERENCE.
Turkish trenches
Turkish wire
Windmill
Heights in feet.

Sketch 9.

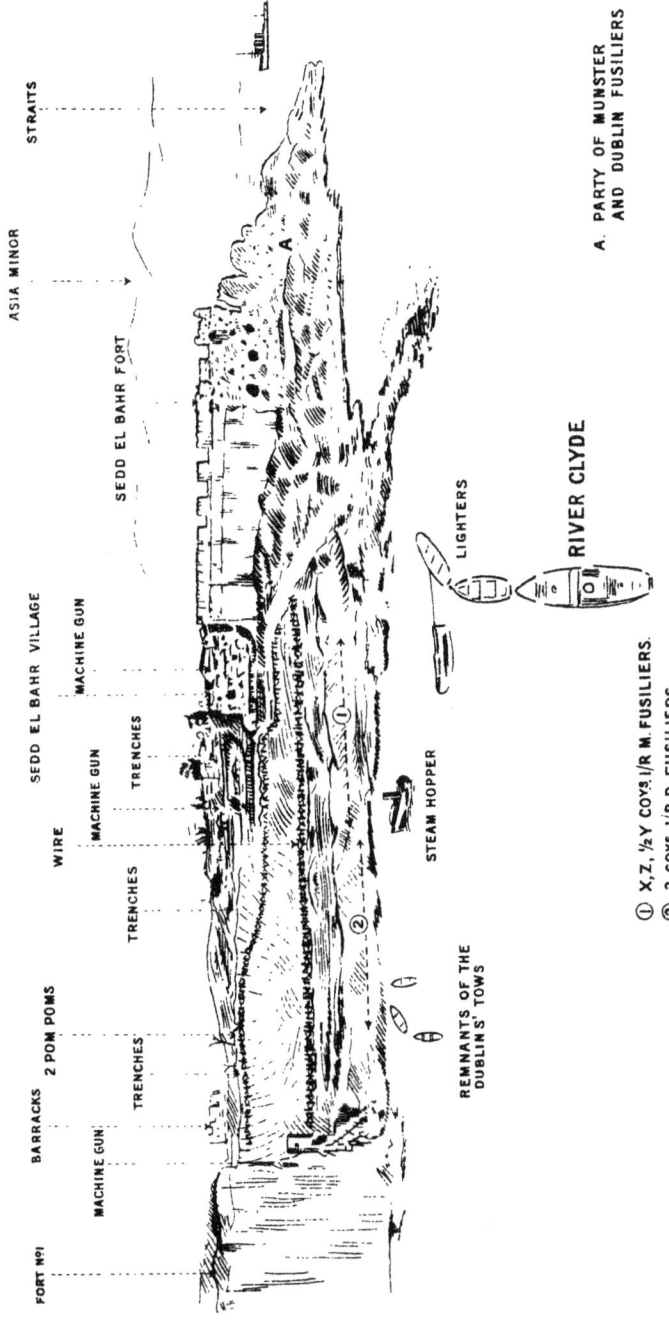

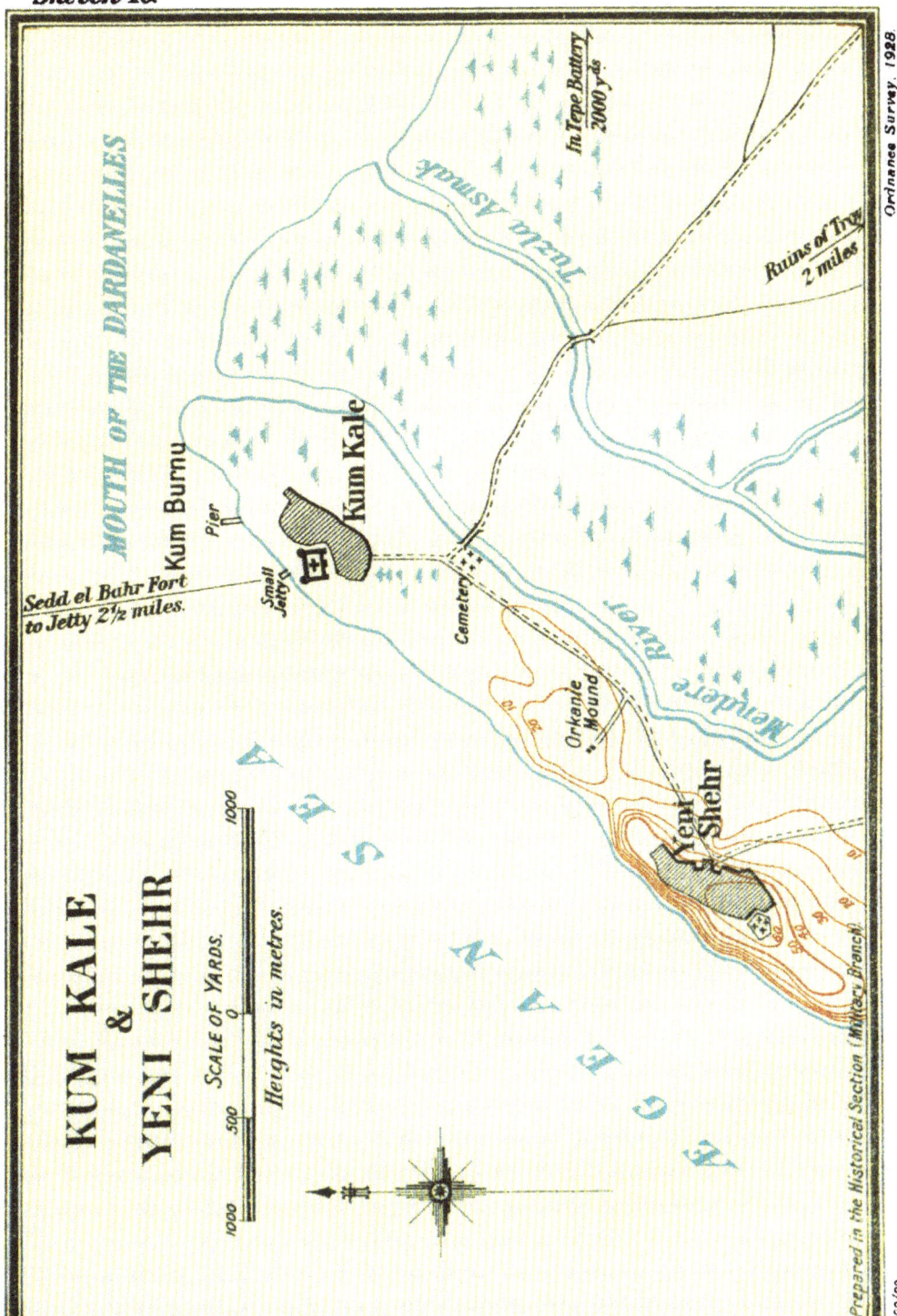

Sketch II

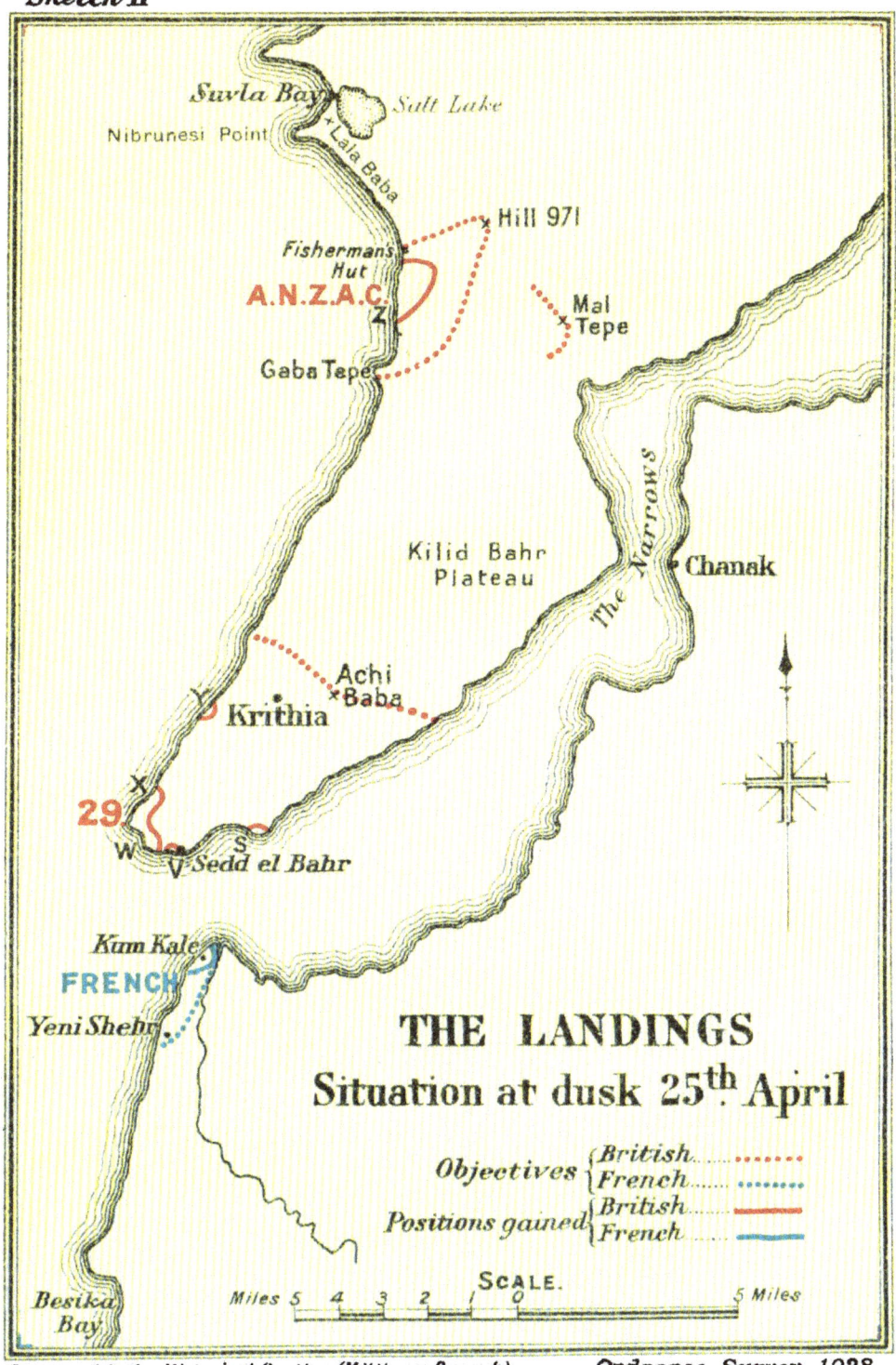

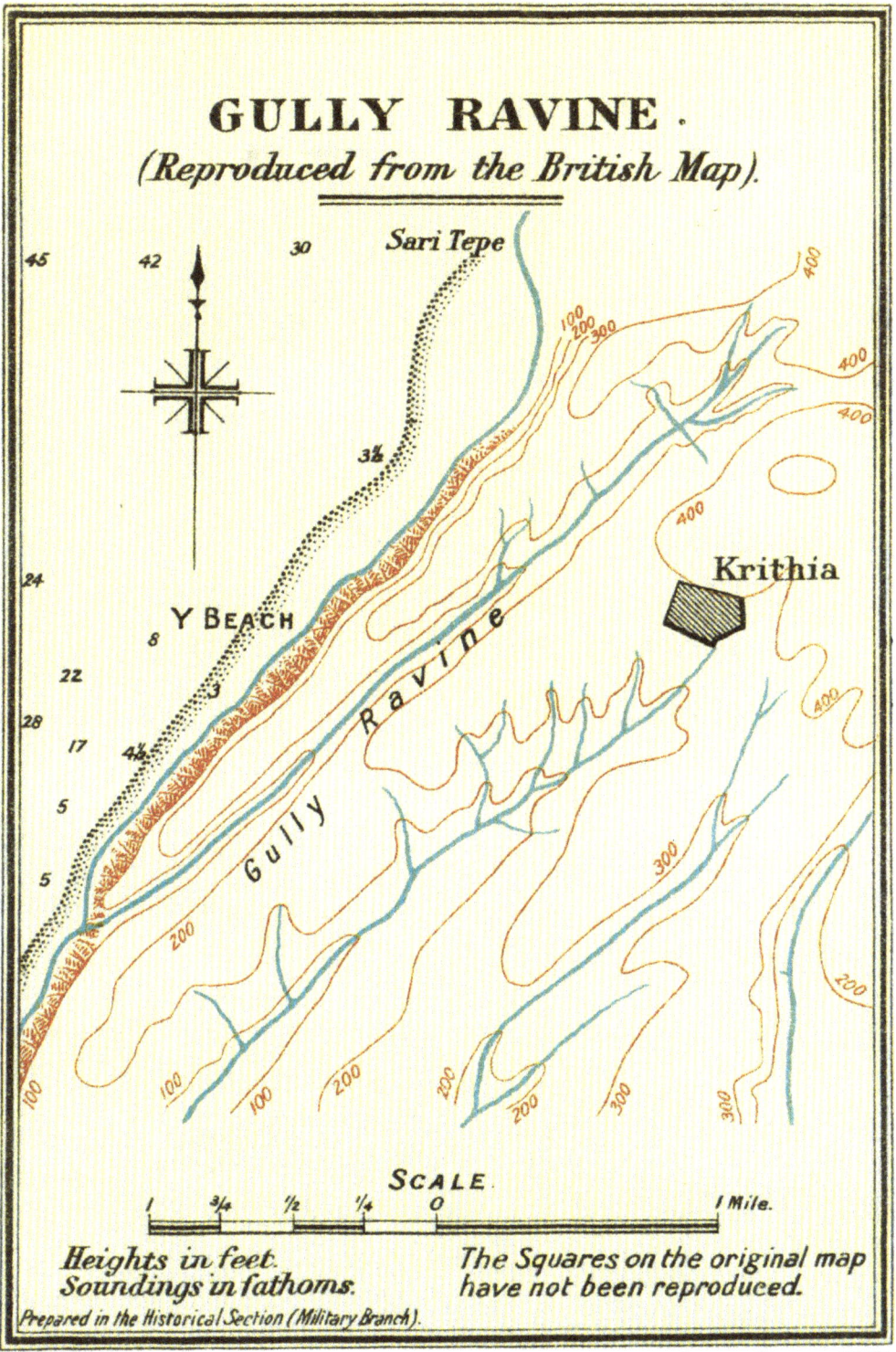

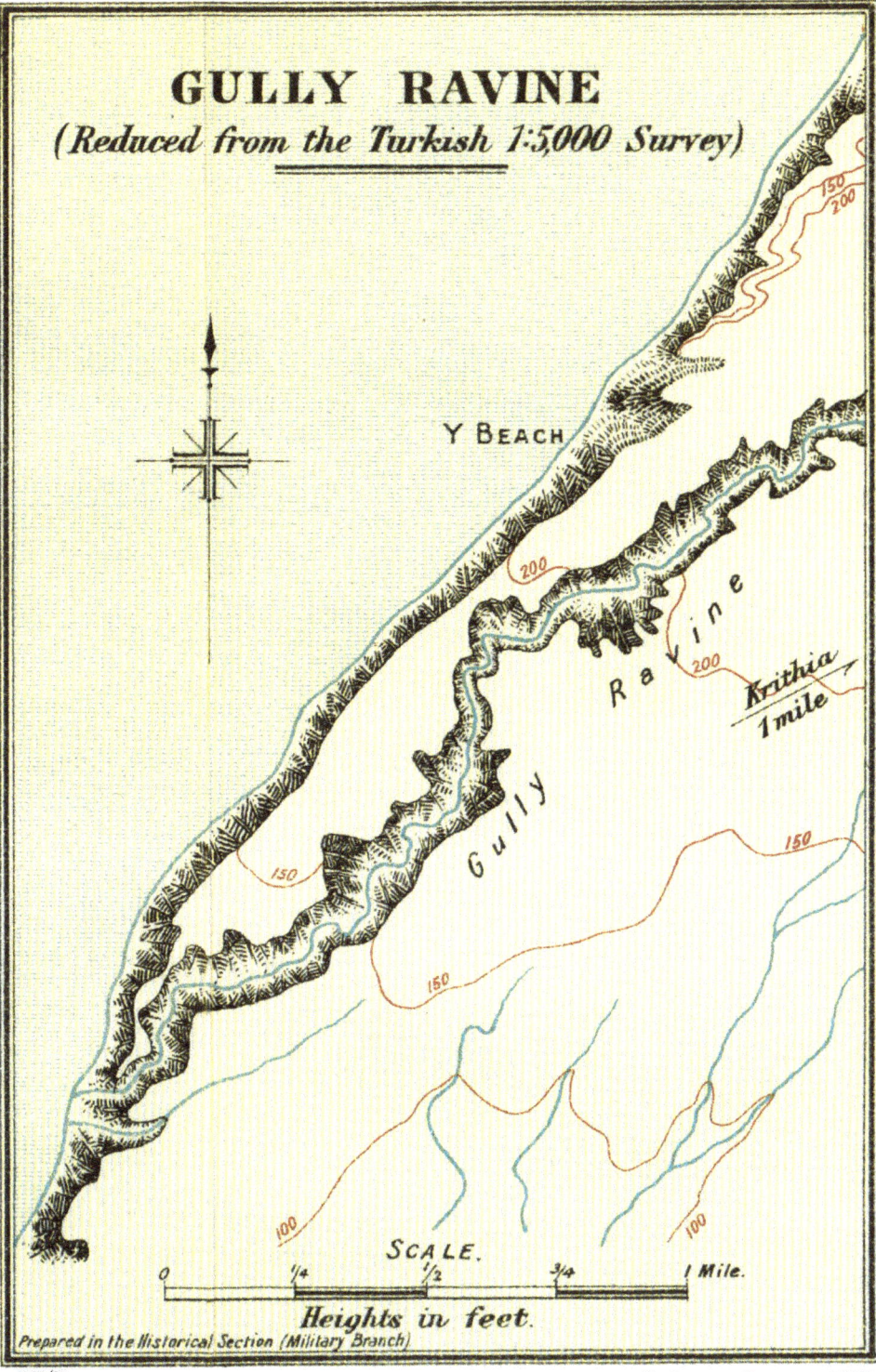

Sketch 14.

FIRST BATTLE OF KRITHIA,
Allied Objectives for 28th April.

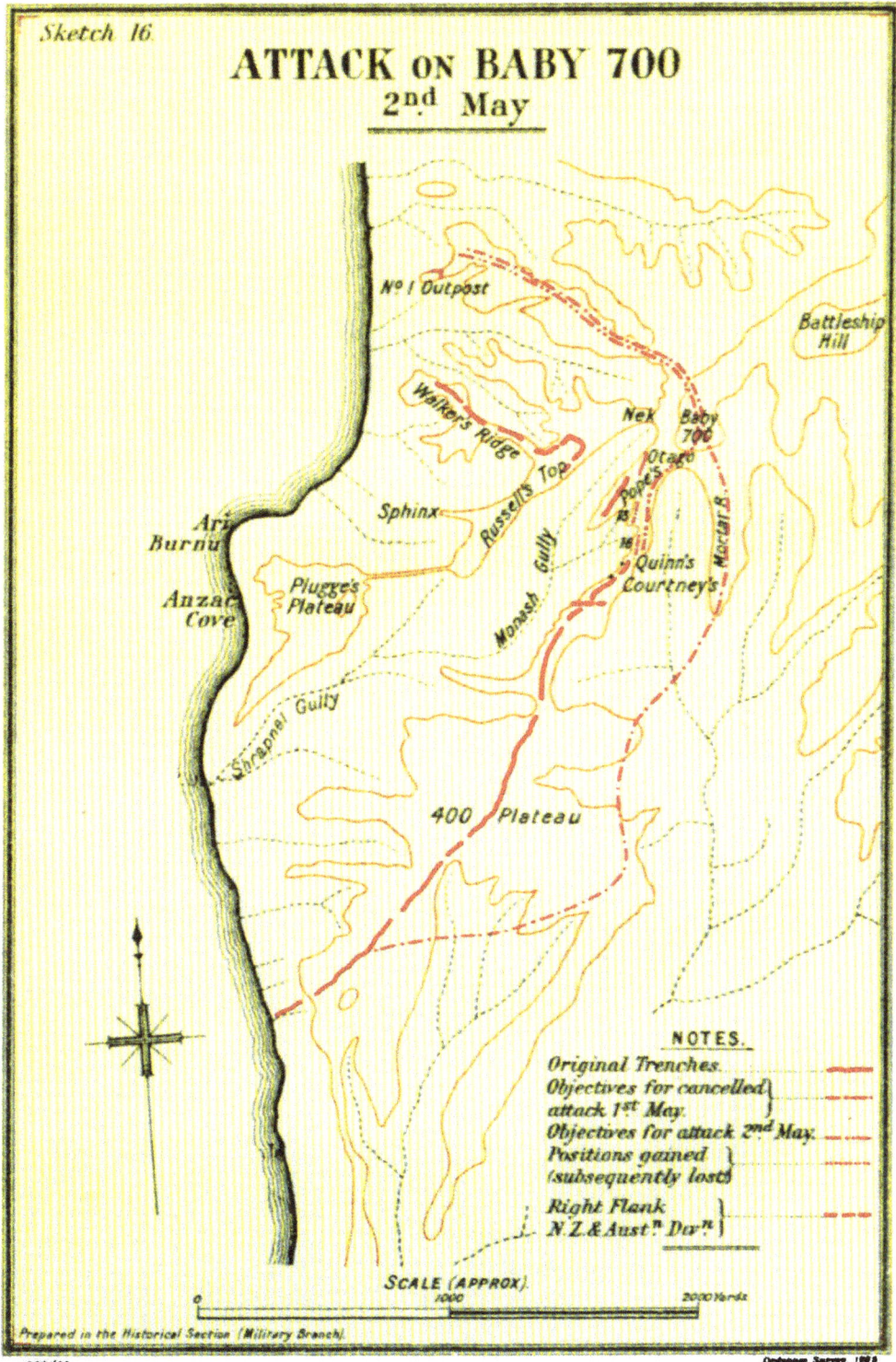

Sketch 17.

TURKISH NIGHT ATTACK
1st/2nd May

British Red. French Blue. Turks Green.
Heights in metres

Prepared in the Historical Section (Military Branch)
Ordnance Survey. 1928.

Sketch 18.

OBJECTIVES
FOR THE
SECOND BATTLE OF KRITHIA

NOTES.

Allied line before the Battle ....
I Objective ....
II Objective ....
III Objective ....
Pivotal Point .... A

British Red. French Blue

Heights of Layers in metres.
(Hills at Helles and Sedd el Bahr in feet.)

Ordnance Survey, 1928.

Prepared in the Historical Section (Military Branch).

Sketch 19.

THE SECOND BATTLE OF KRITHIA
6th — 8th May

NOTES.

Turkish trenches located before the battle.
1st Objective 6th May.
Approximate Allied line night 5th/6th May.
Approximate Position reached 6th May.
Approximate Position reached 7th May.
Approximate Position reached 8th May.
British–Red. French & 2nd Naval Brigade–Blue.

SCALE OF MILES.

Prepared in the Historical Section (Military Branch.)

Ordnance Survey, 1928.

HISTORY OF THE GREAT WAR

BASED ON OFFICIAL DOCUMENTS
BY DIRECTION OF THE HISTORICAL SECTION
COMMITTEE OF IMPERIAL DEFENCE

MILITARY OPERATIONS

GALLIPOLI

ATLAS

MAPS AND SKETCHES COMPILED BY
MAJOR A. F. BECKE
R.A. (RETIRED), HON. M.A. (OXON.)

VOL. II
MAY 1915 TO THE EVACUATION

The Naval & Military Press Ltd

SKETCHES

[*N.B.*—The spelling of the place-names in the Sketches and Maps agrees with the rulings, where such have been given, of the Royal Geographical Society's Permanent Committee on Geographical Names.]

A. Suvla

1. Anzac: Opposing Lines towards end of May
2. Section of Gallipoli Peninsula on line attacked 4th June
3. Third Battle of Krithia: Opposing Lines, 4th June
4. Third Battle of Krithia: Situation 8 A.M. 4th June
5. Third Battle of Krithia: Result
6. Battle of 21st June: French Objectives
7. Gully Ravine: Opposing Lines, 28th June
8. Gully Ravine: Result of Battle
9. Battle of 12th/13th July
10. Helles: Opposing Lines, mid-July
11. Objectives for the August Offensive
12. Turkish Dispositions, 6th August
13. Battle of 6th/7th August at Helles
14. Lone Pine, 6th August
15. Lone Pine after Consolidation
16. Battle of Sari Bair: Opposing Lines, 6th August, and British Objectives
17. Battle of Sari Bair: Situation, Evening 7th August
18. Battle of Sari Bair: Objectives, 8th August
19. Battle of Sari Bair: Situation, Evening 8th August

GALLIPOLI

20. Battle of Sari Bair: Situation 5 A.M. 9th August
21. Suvla: Turkish Defences reported to Gen. Stopford, 6th August
22. Suvla: Turkish Dispositions, 6th August
23. Suvla: Situation 8 A.M. 7th August
24. Suvla: Situation 1 A.M. 8th August
25. Suvla: Situation 7 P.M. 8th August
26. Suvla: Situation 7 P.M. 9th August
27. Battle of Sari Bair: Situation, Dawn 10th August
28. Battle of Sari Bair: Opposing Front Lines after Battle
29. Scimitar Hill, 21st August
30. Hill 60, 21st August
31. Evacuation of Anzac, 19th/20th Dec.
32. Evacuation of Suvla, 19th/20th Dec.
33. Evacuation of Helles, 8th/9th Jan. 1916
33A. Evacuation of Helles: 52nd Division Arrangements, 8th Jan. 1916

Sketch A.

SUVLA

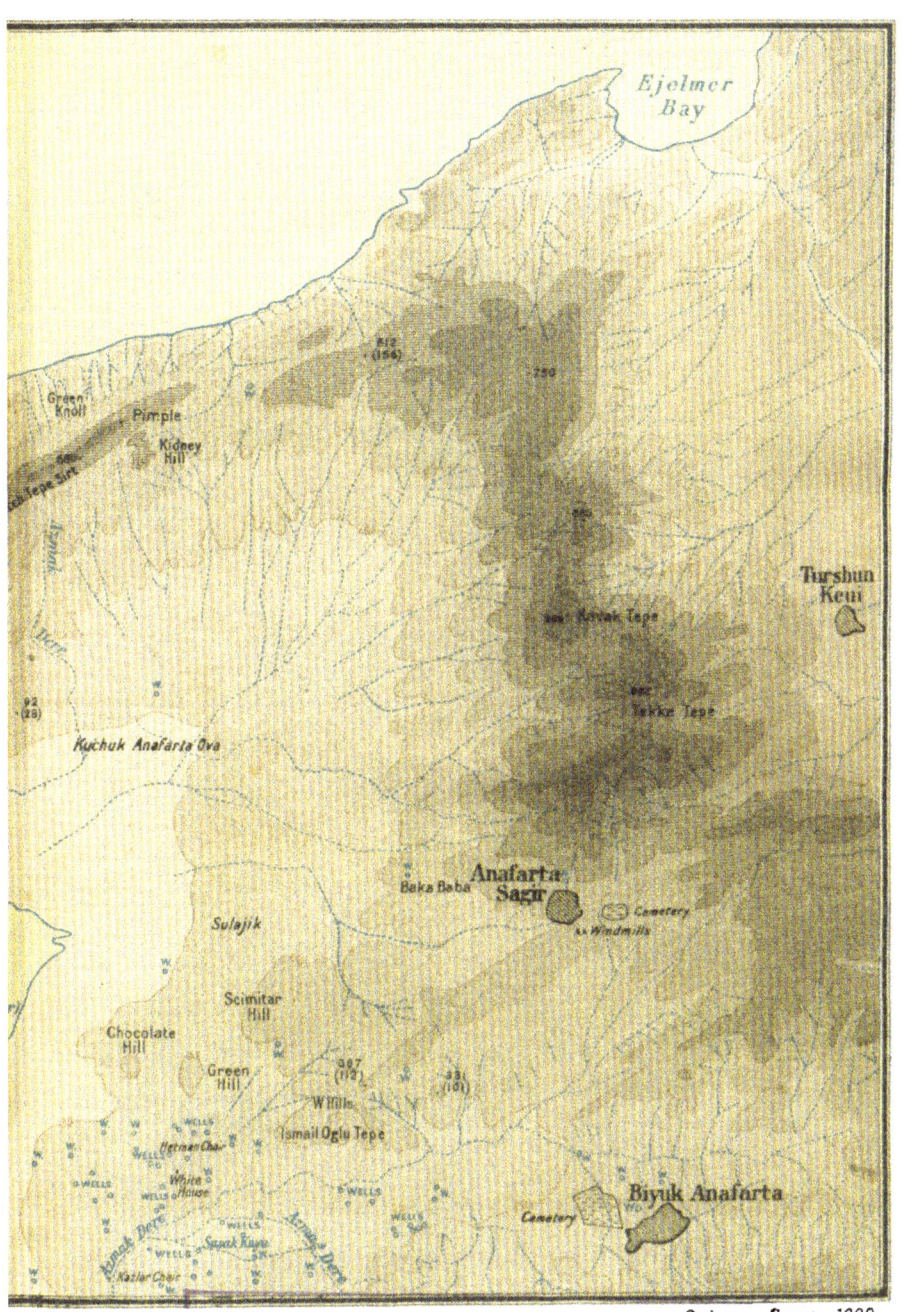

Ordnance Survey, 1929.

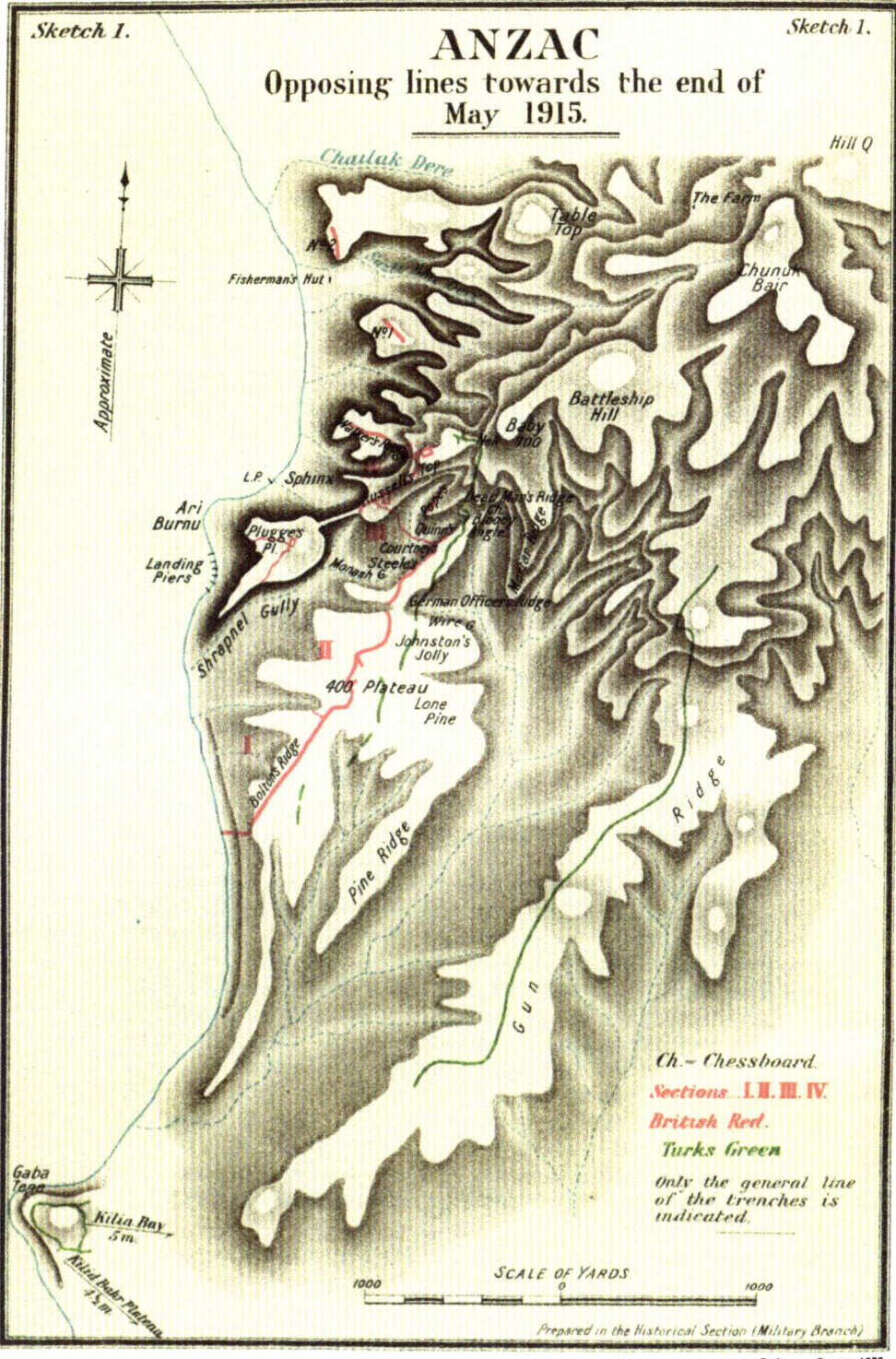

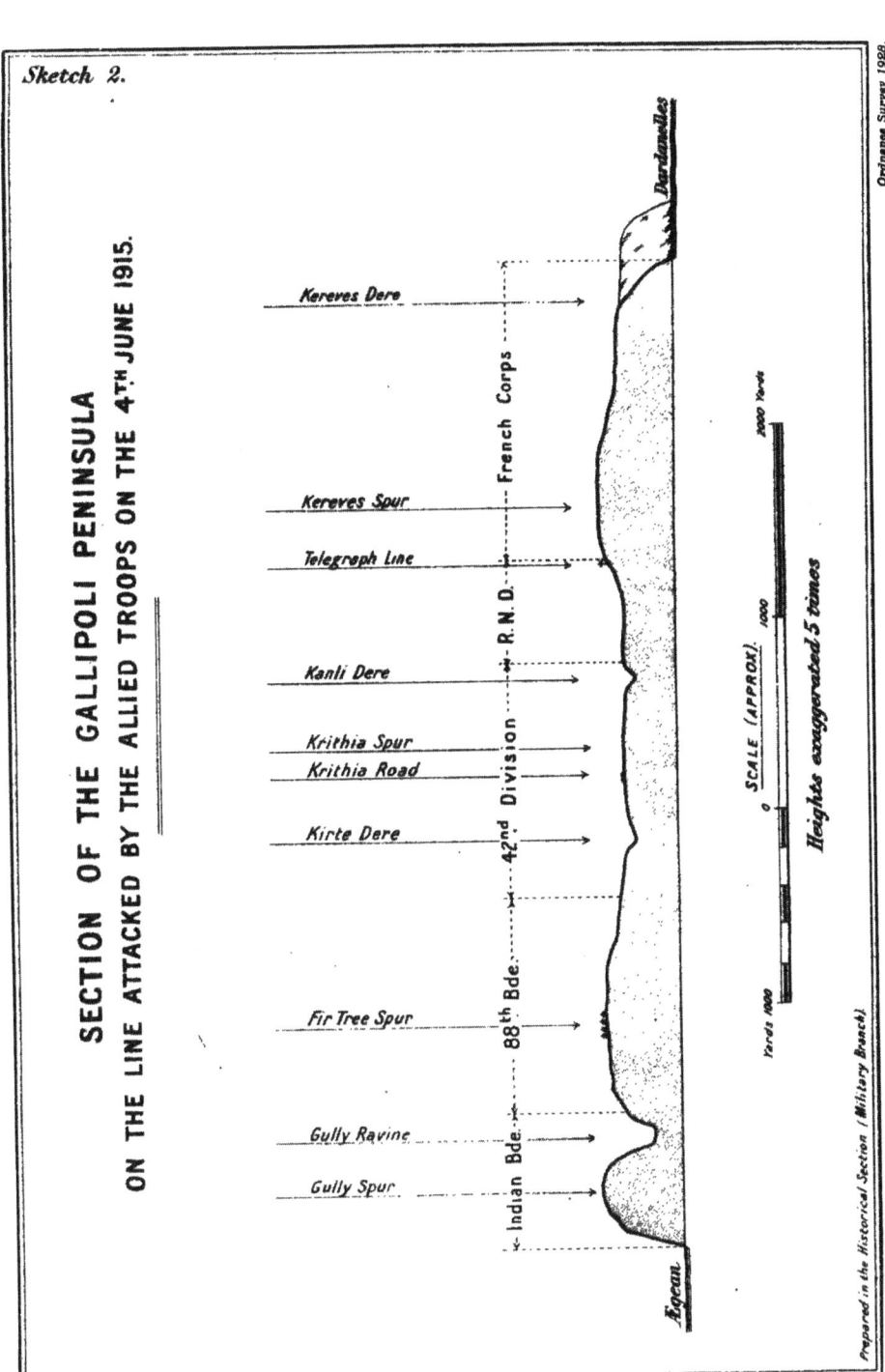

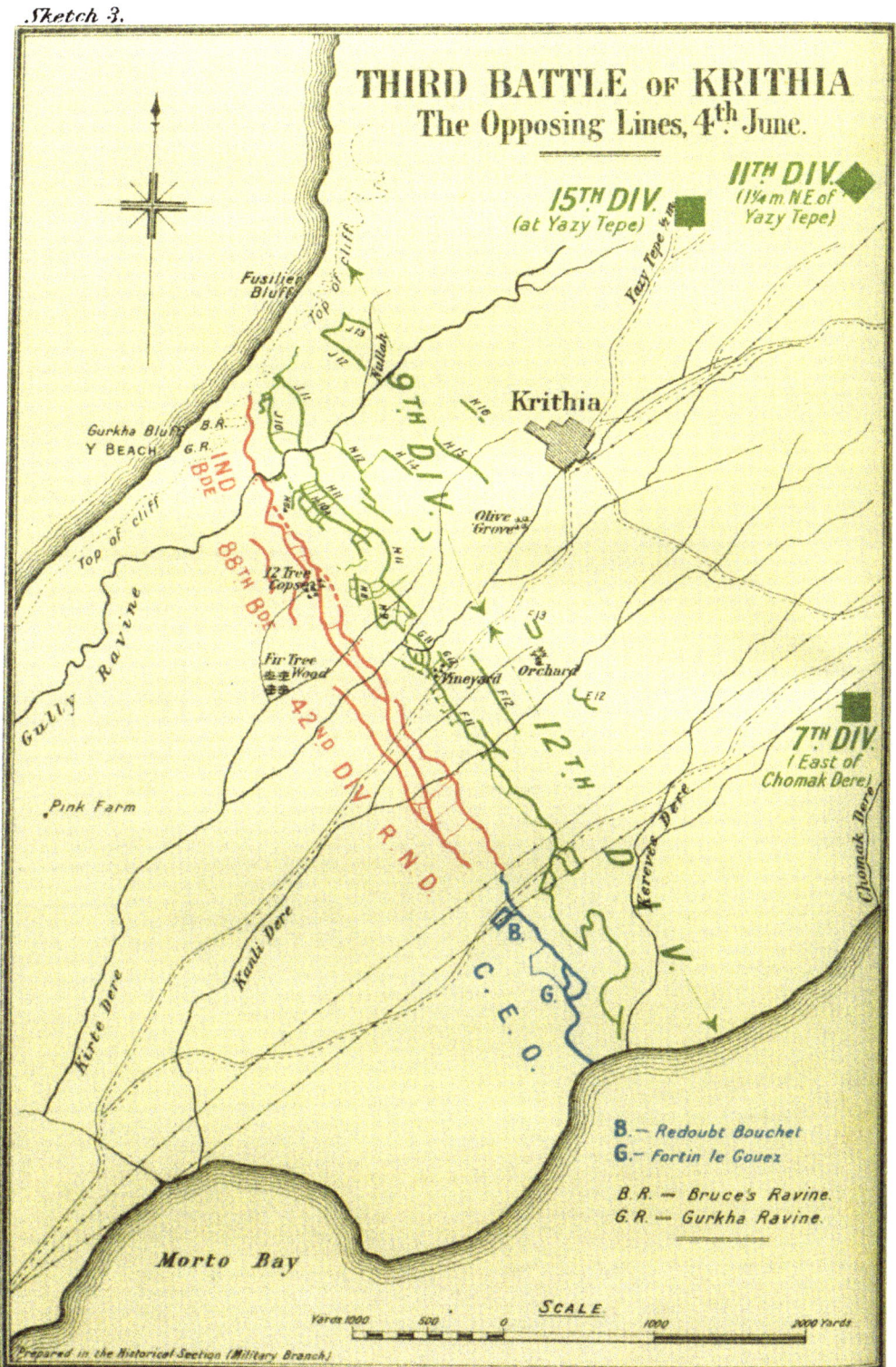

Sketch 4.

THIRD BATTLE OF KRITHIA
Situation, 8 a.m. 4th June.

NOTES.

Turks ....
French ....
British ....
Battalions in Corps Reserve ■

Heights of Layers in metres
(Hills at Helles and Sedd el Bahr in feet.)

Prepared in the Historical Section (Military Branch).

Ordnance Survey, 1928.

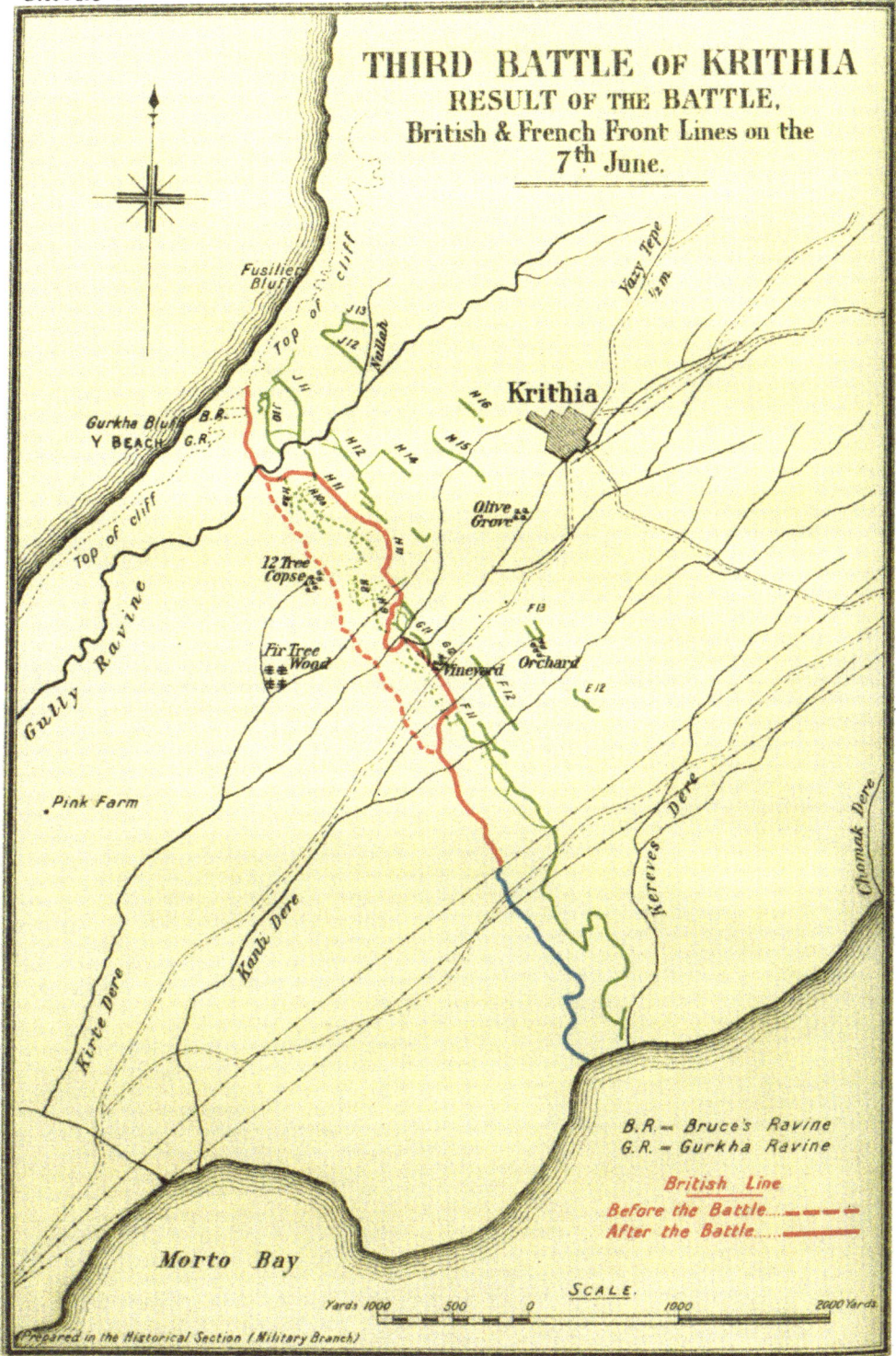

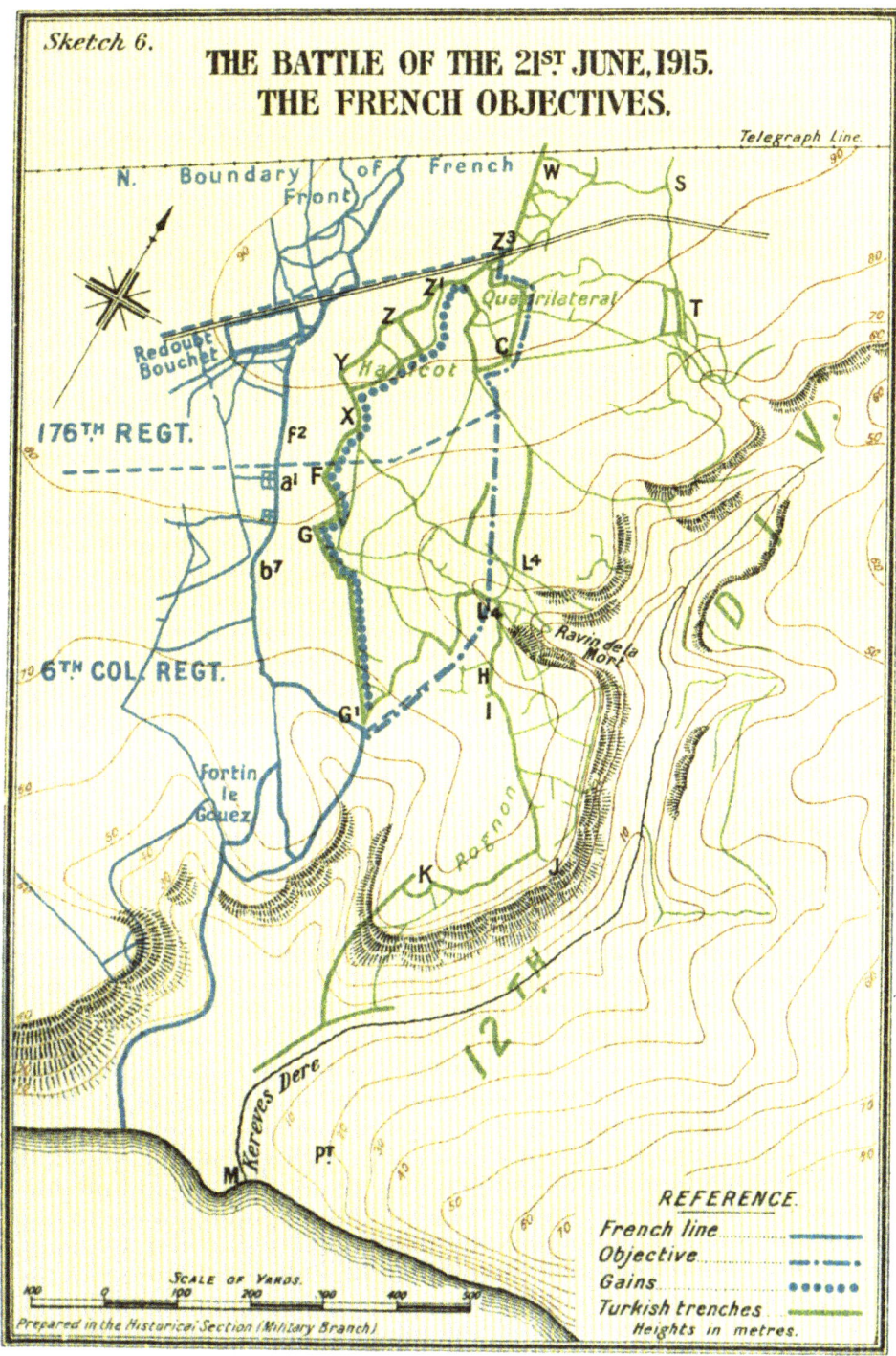

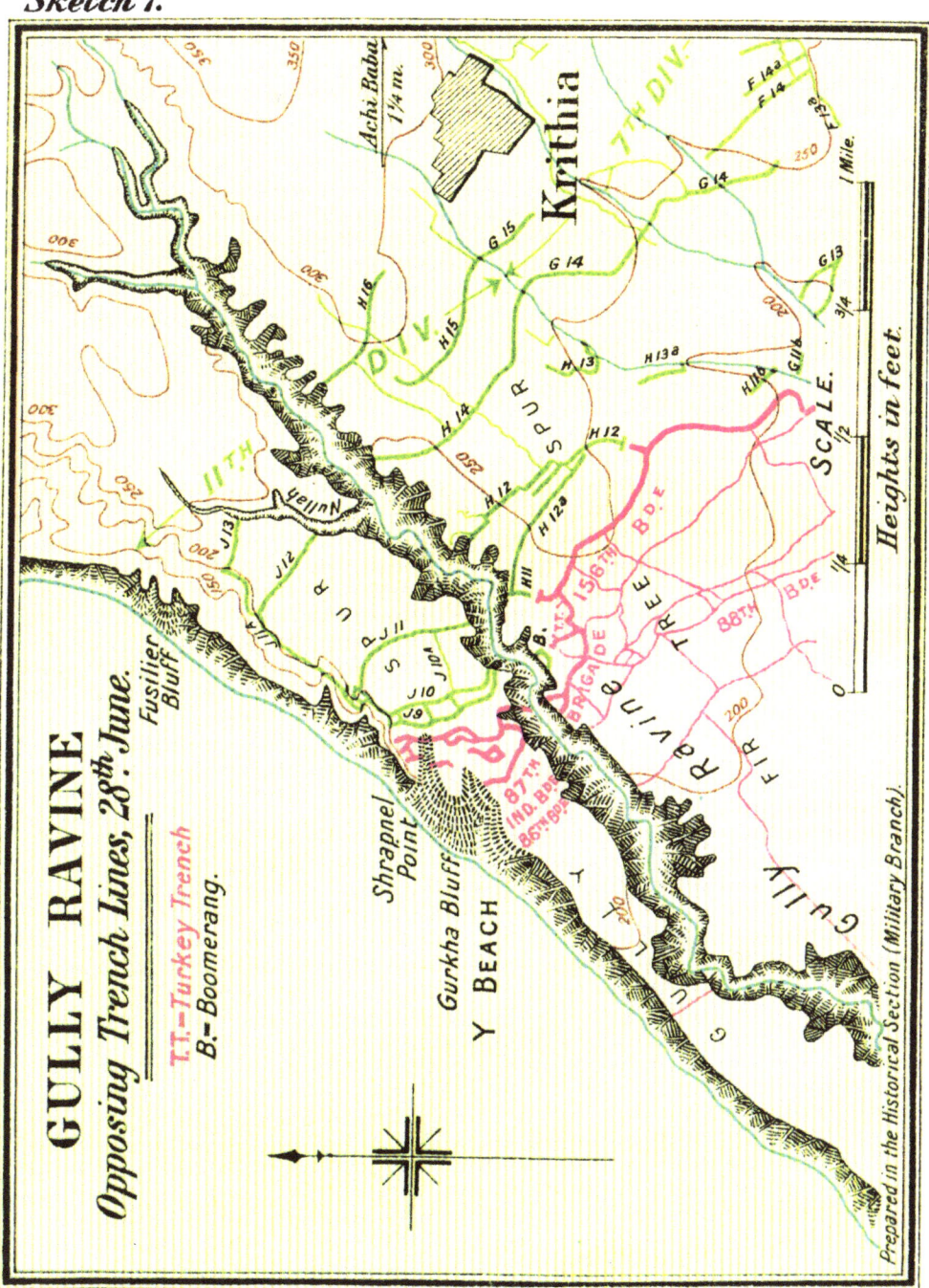

Sketch 8.

GULLY RAVINE
28th June – 5th July
Result of the Battle.

Sketch 9.

THE BATTLE OF THE 12TH/13TH JULY 1915.

REFERENCE
Allied Positions, Dawn 12th July ————
Allied Objectives ————
Allied Positions, Dawn 14th July • • • •
Brigade Boundaries ————
Shallow or uncompleted Turkish Trenches - - - -
Heights in Feet.

Ordnance Survey 1929.

Sketch 10.

HELLES
The Result of the Fighting from June 28th to July 13th
The Opposing Lines in mid-July.

Line before the attacks ....
Line at the end of the fighting ....

SCALE.
Yards 1000   500   0   1000   2000 Yards

Prepared in the Historical Section (Military Branch).

Ordnance Survey 1929.

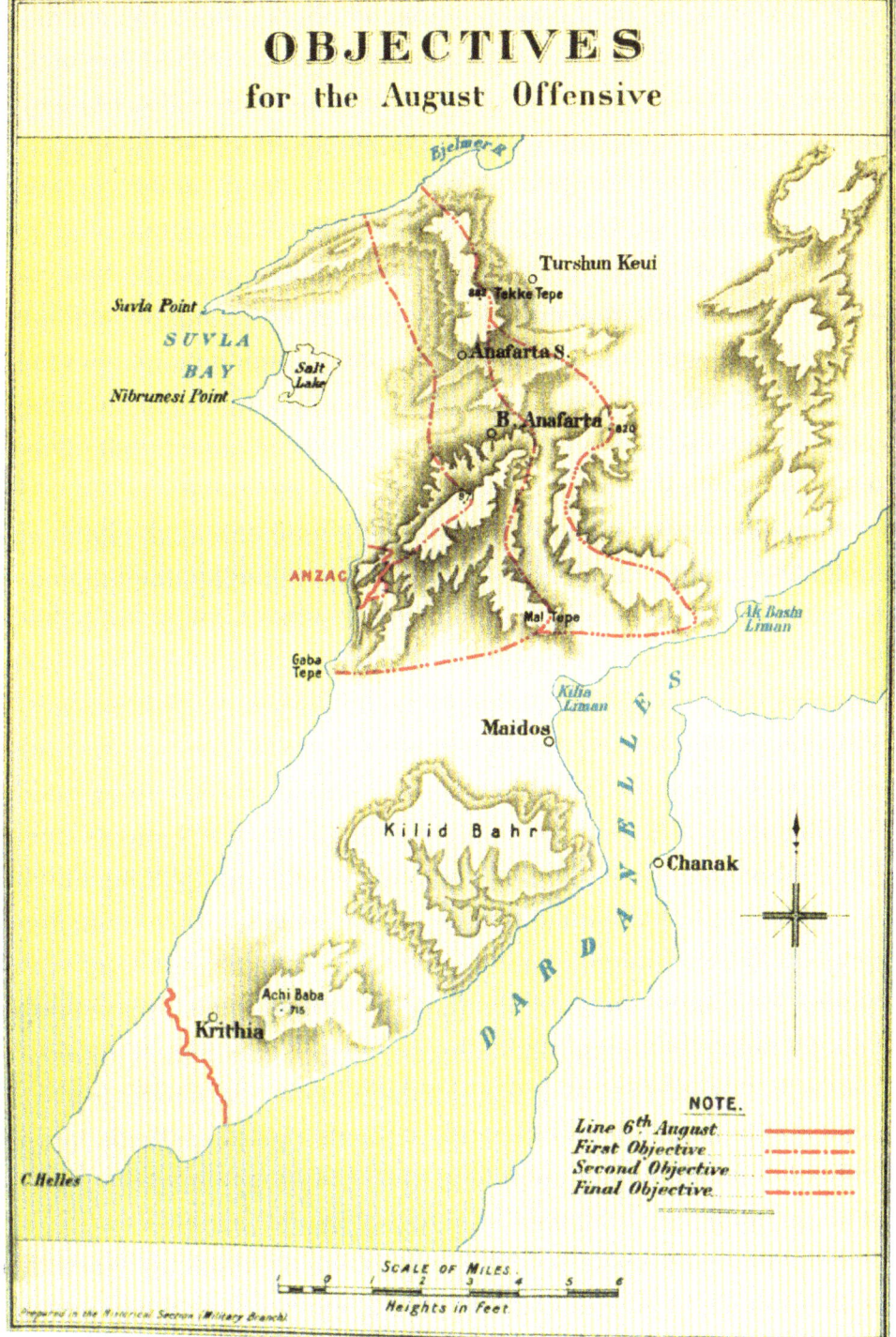

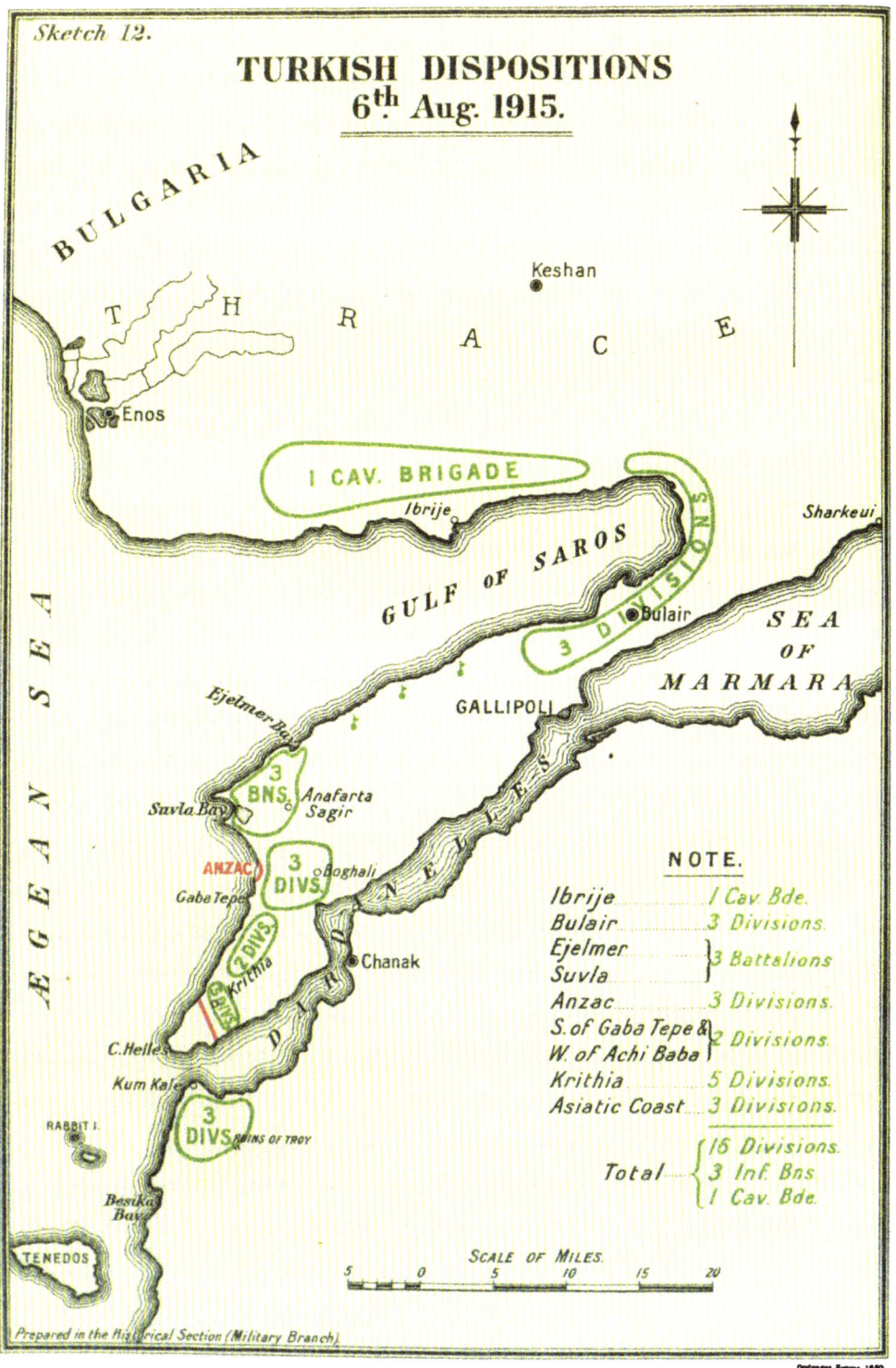

Sketch 13.

THE BATTLE OF 6TH/7TH AUGUST AT HELLES.

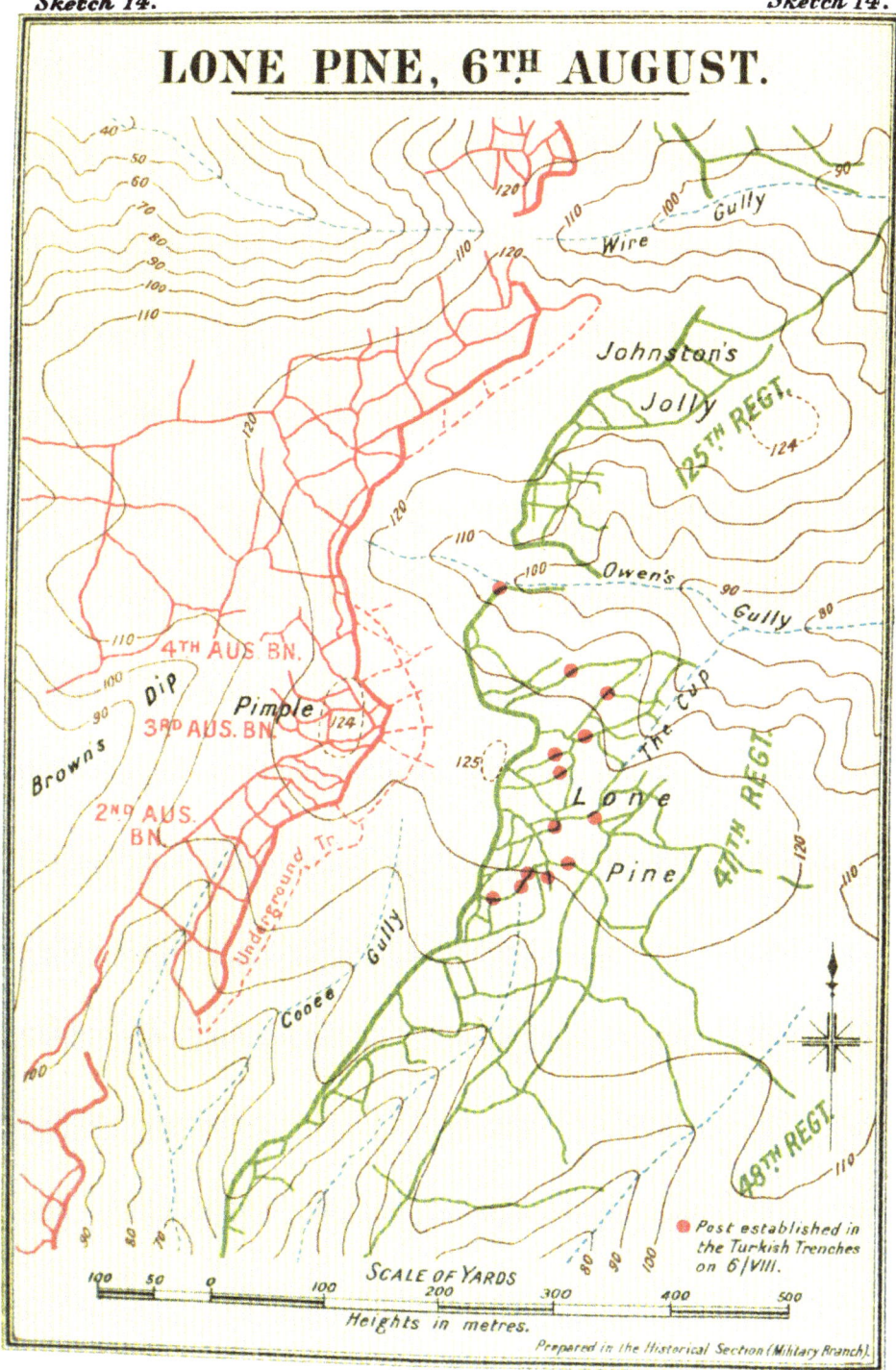

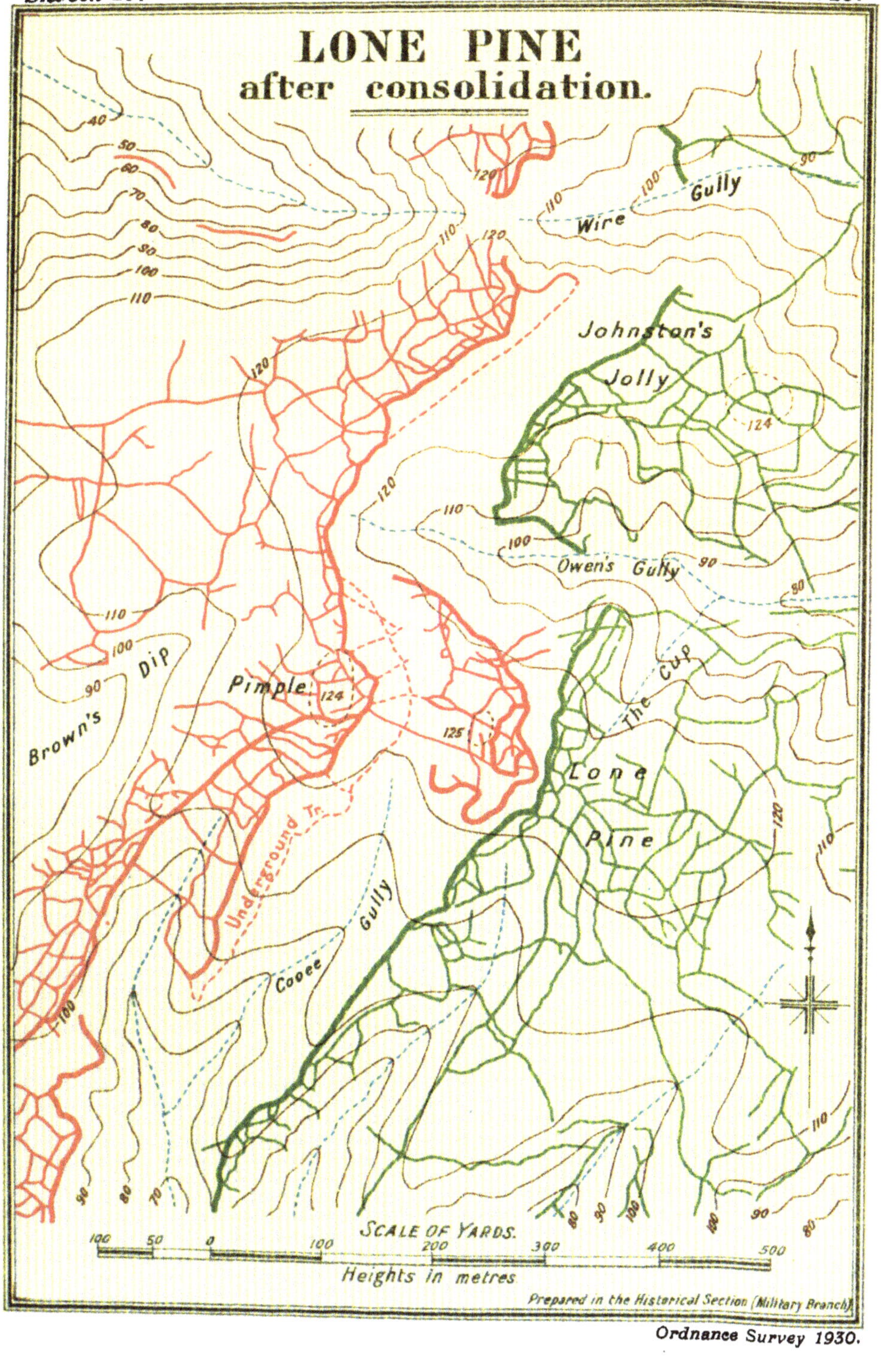

Ordnance Survey 1930.

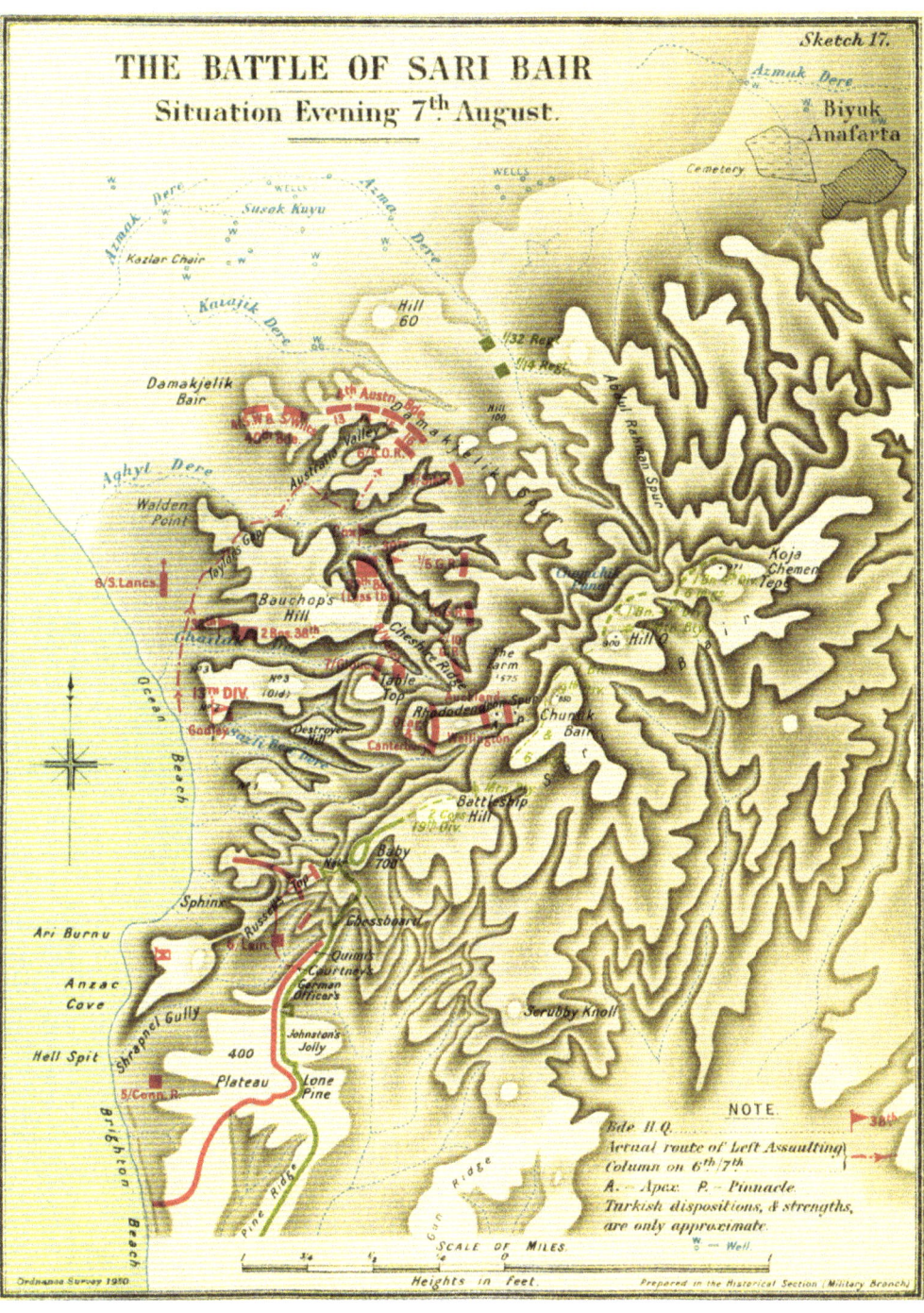

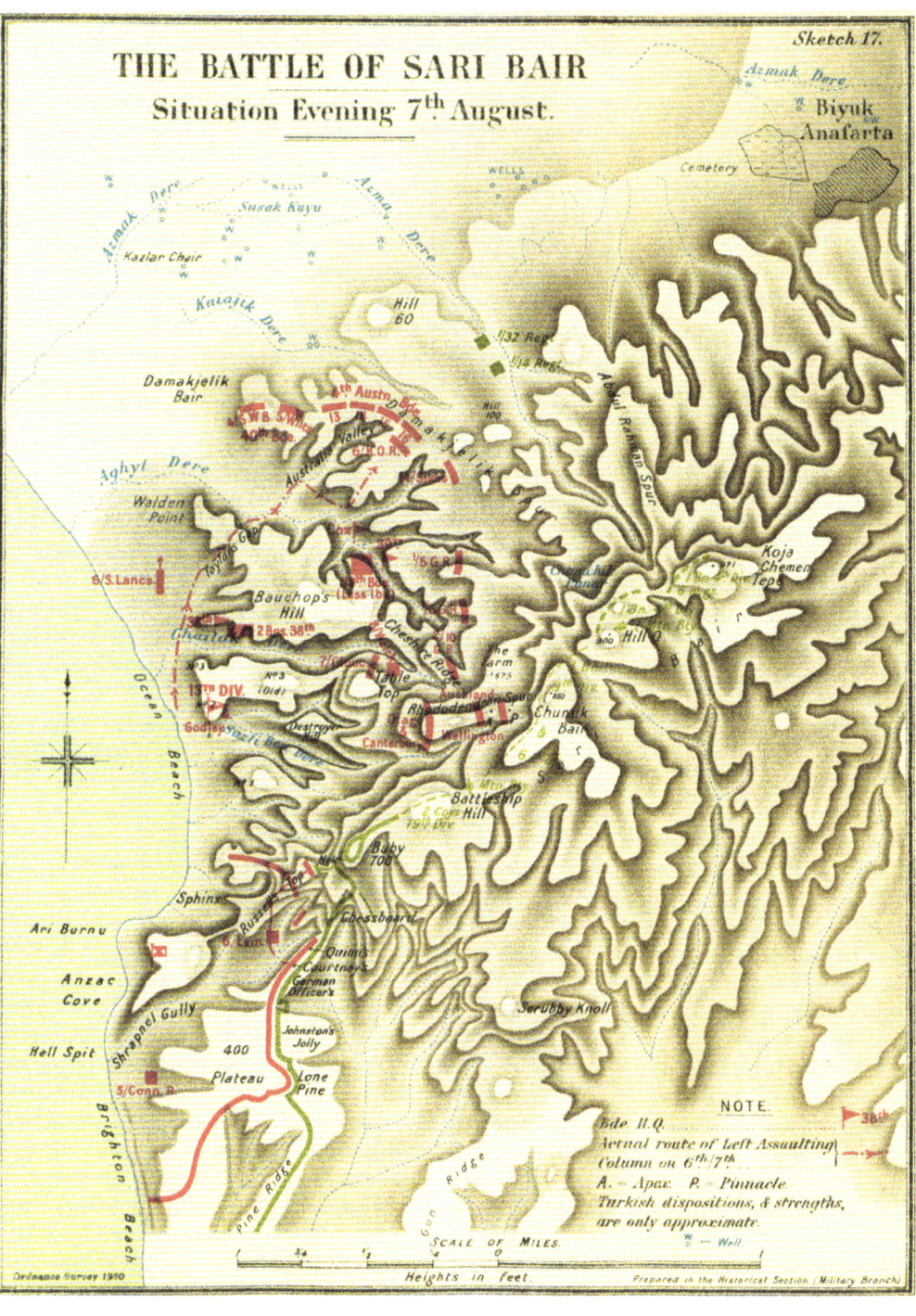

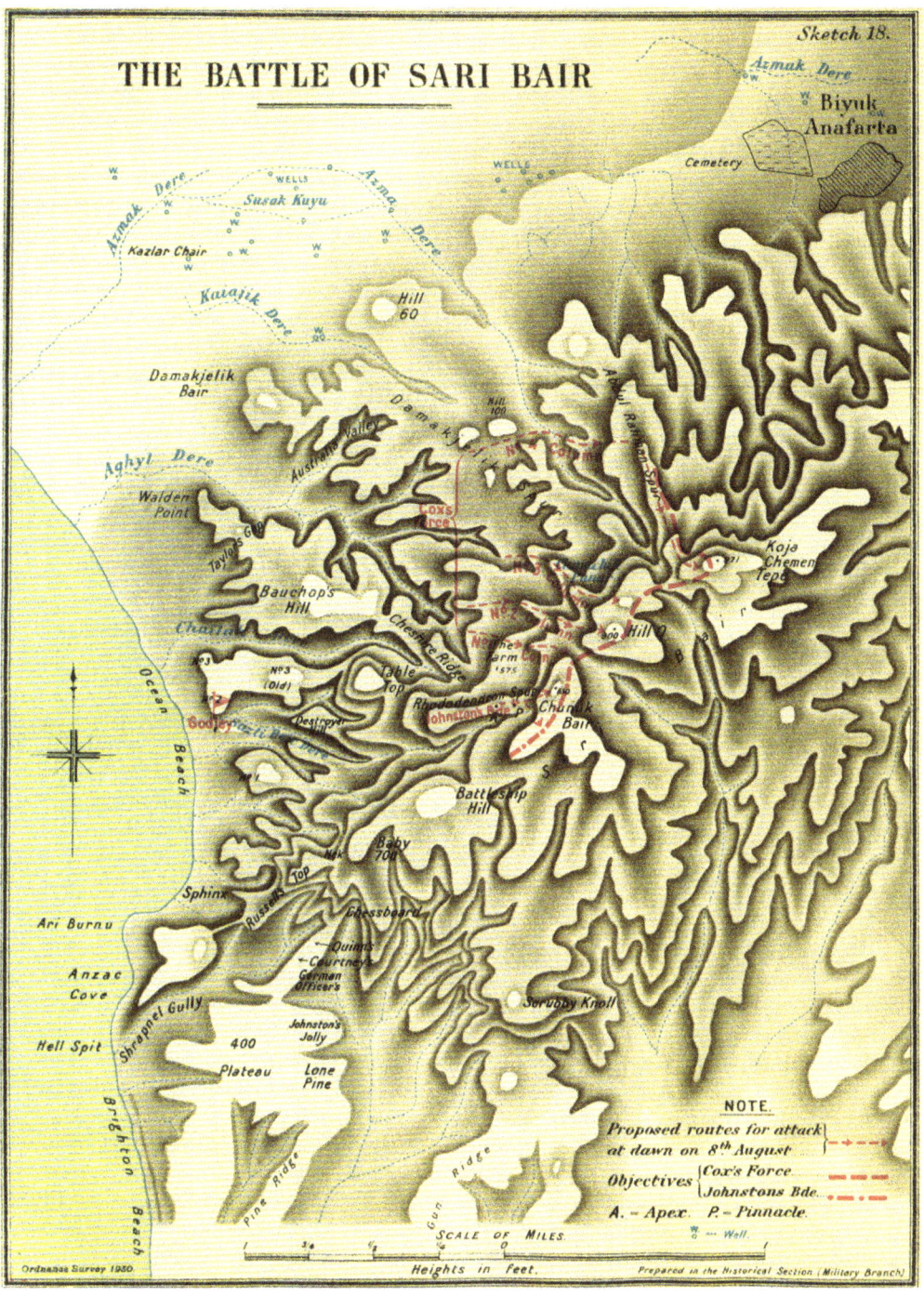

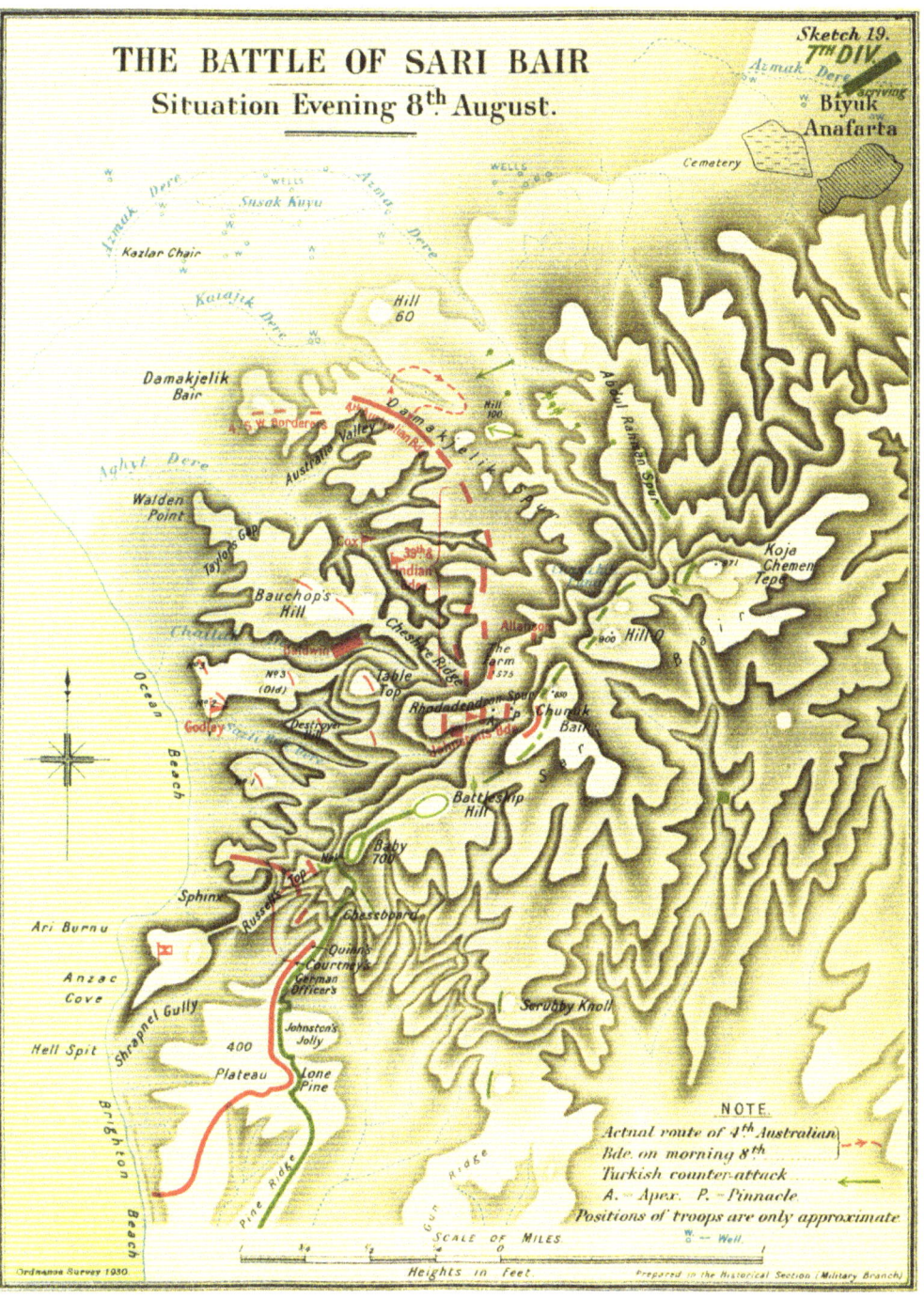

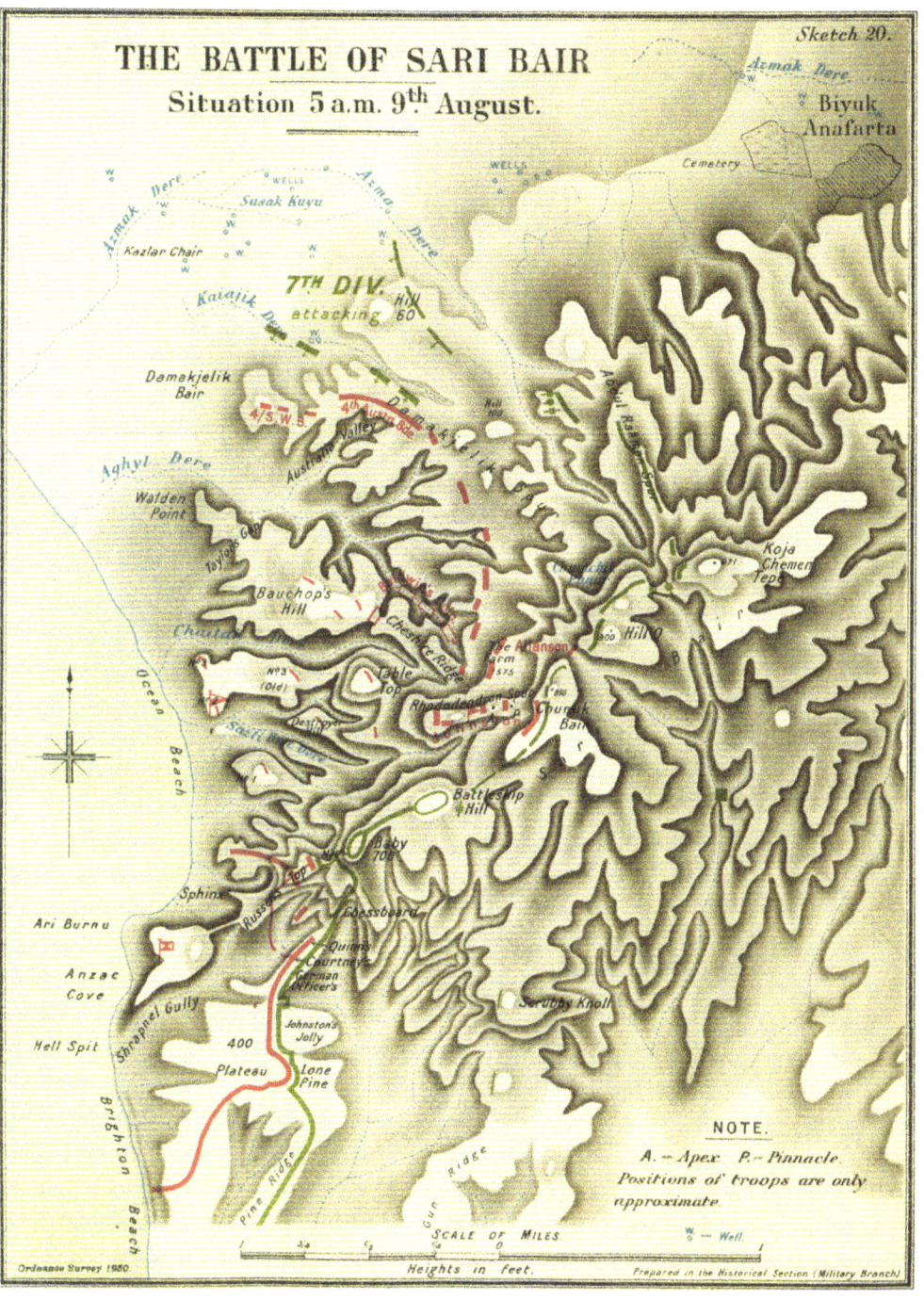

Sketch 21.

SUVLA, 1915.
Turkish Defences as reported to General Stopford by G.H.Q. on the 6th August.

Sketch 22.

TURKISH DISPOSITIONS AT SUVLA
9.30 p.m. 6th August 1915.

REFERENCE
- ● Sentry Group
- ☐ Platoon
- ■ Company
- Dismtd Cavalry Troop
- Mountain Gun
- Field Gun
- ○ Detachment H.Q.

Sketch 23.

SUVLA
8 a.m., 7th August.

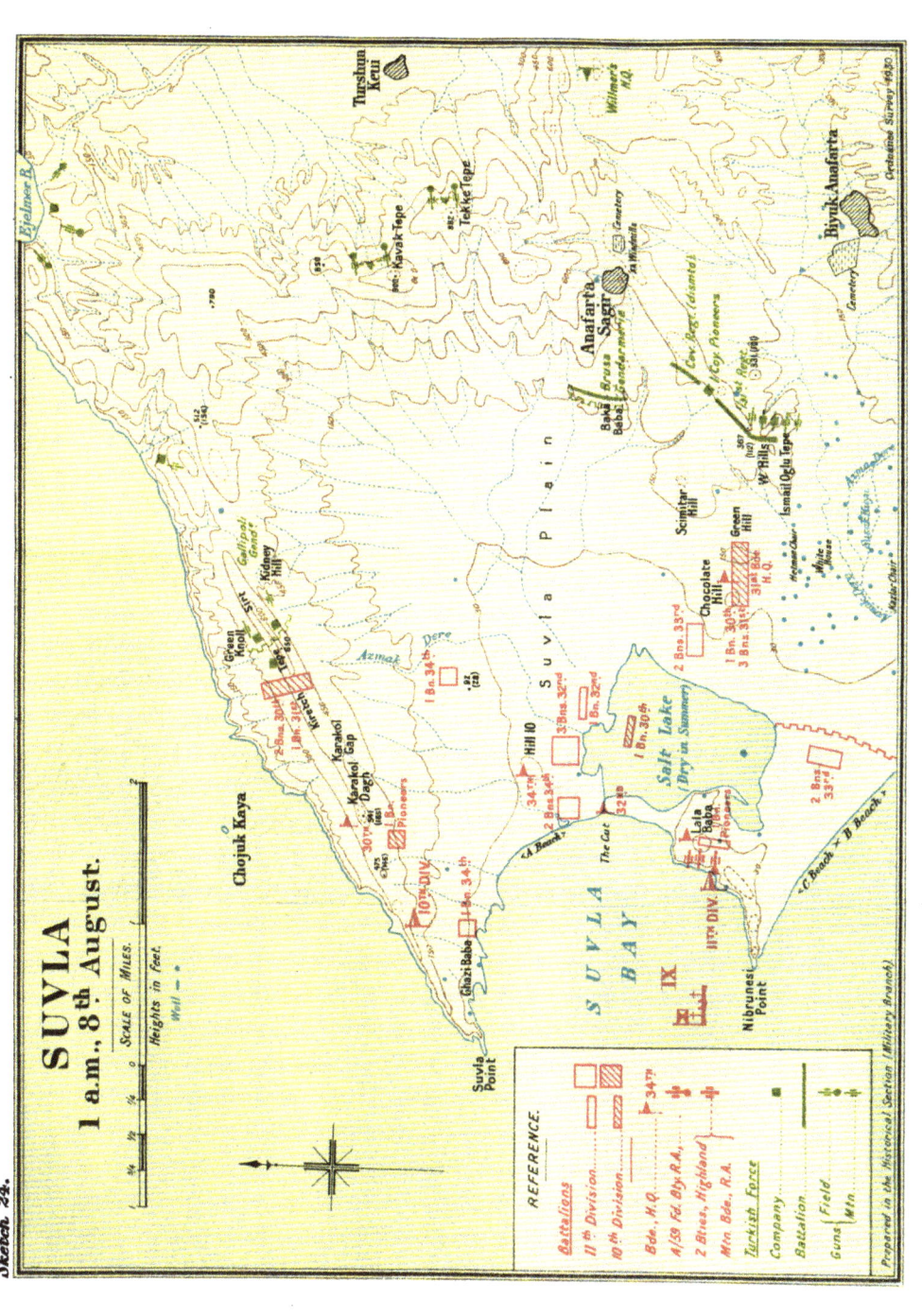

Sketch 25.

SUVLA
7 p.m., 8th August.
Arrival of the Turkish reinforcements.

Sketch 26.

SUVLA
British and Turkish front lines
7 p.m., 9th August.

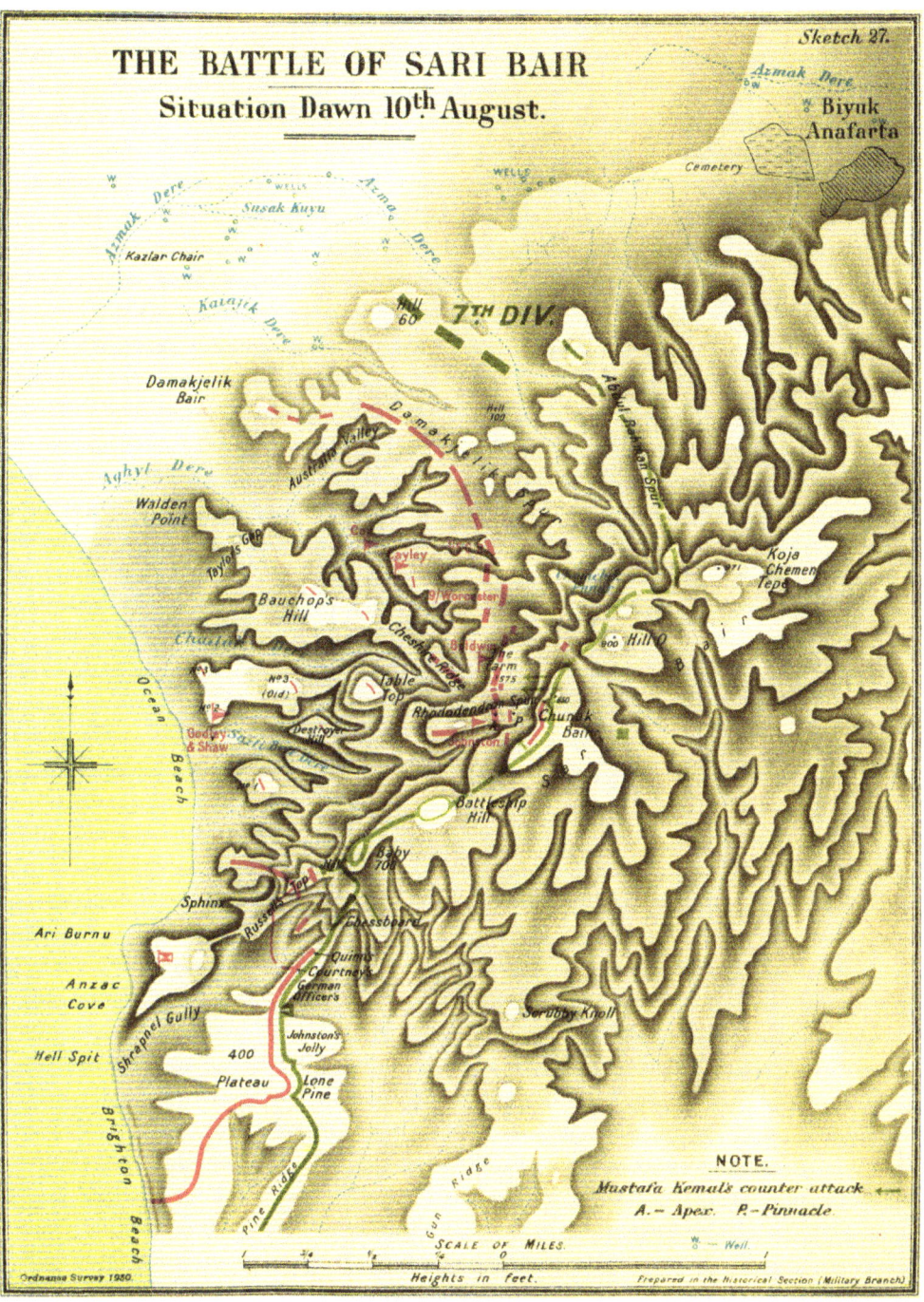

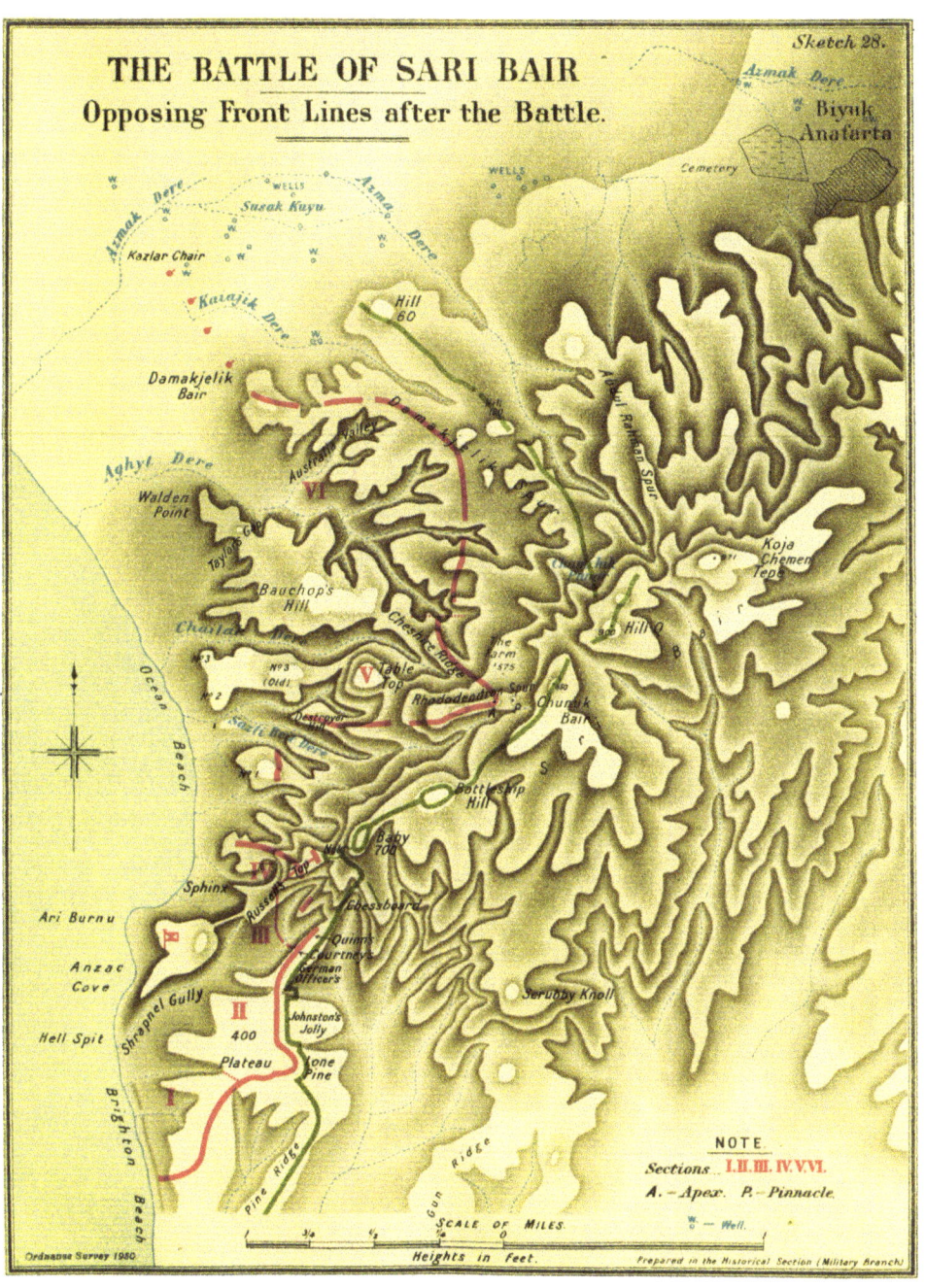

Sketch 29.

SCIMITAR HILL
21st August.

Sketch 30.

HILL 60
21st August.

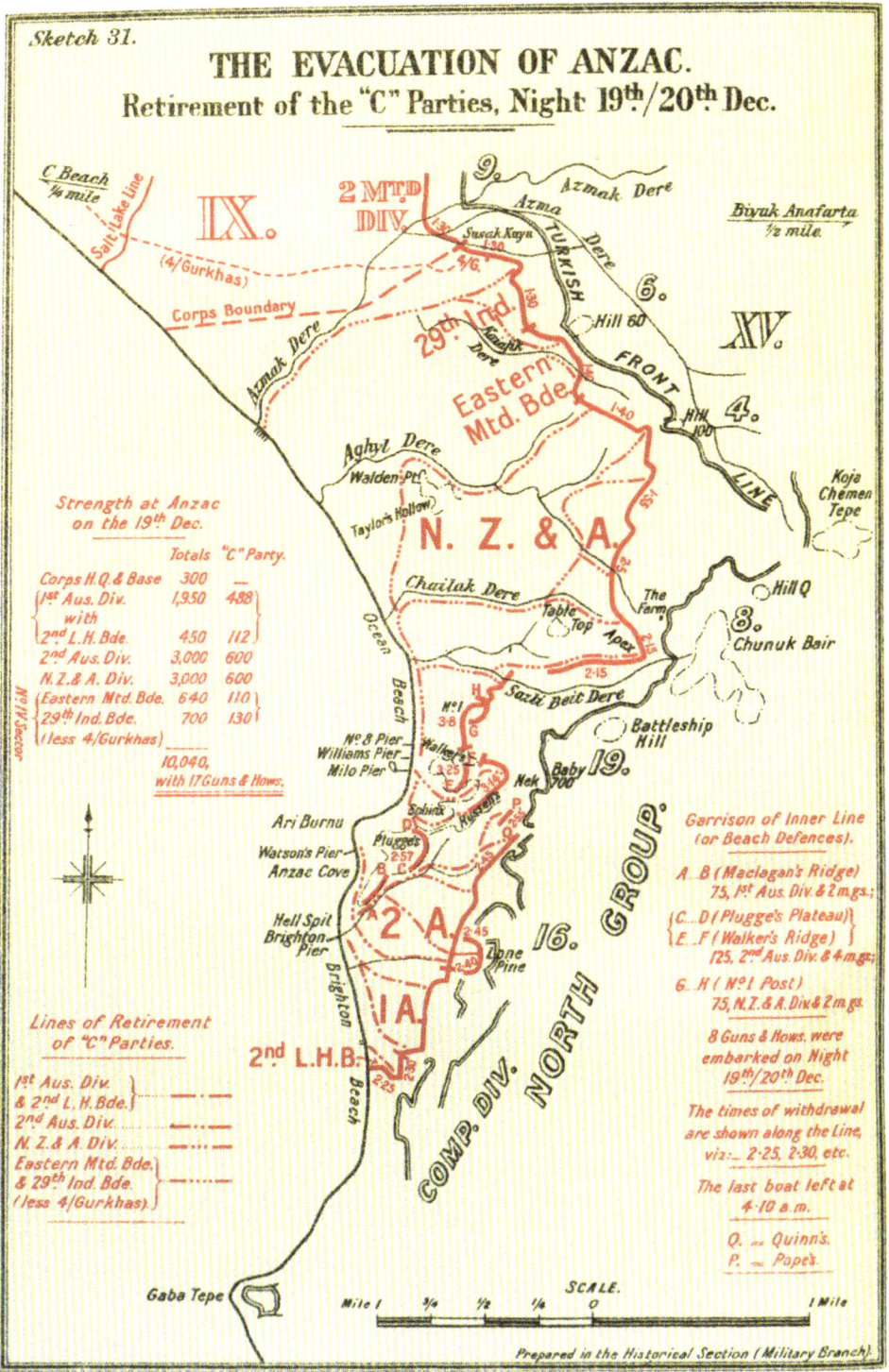

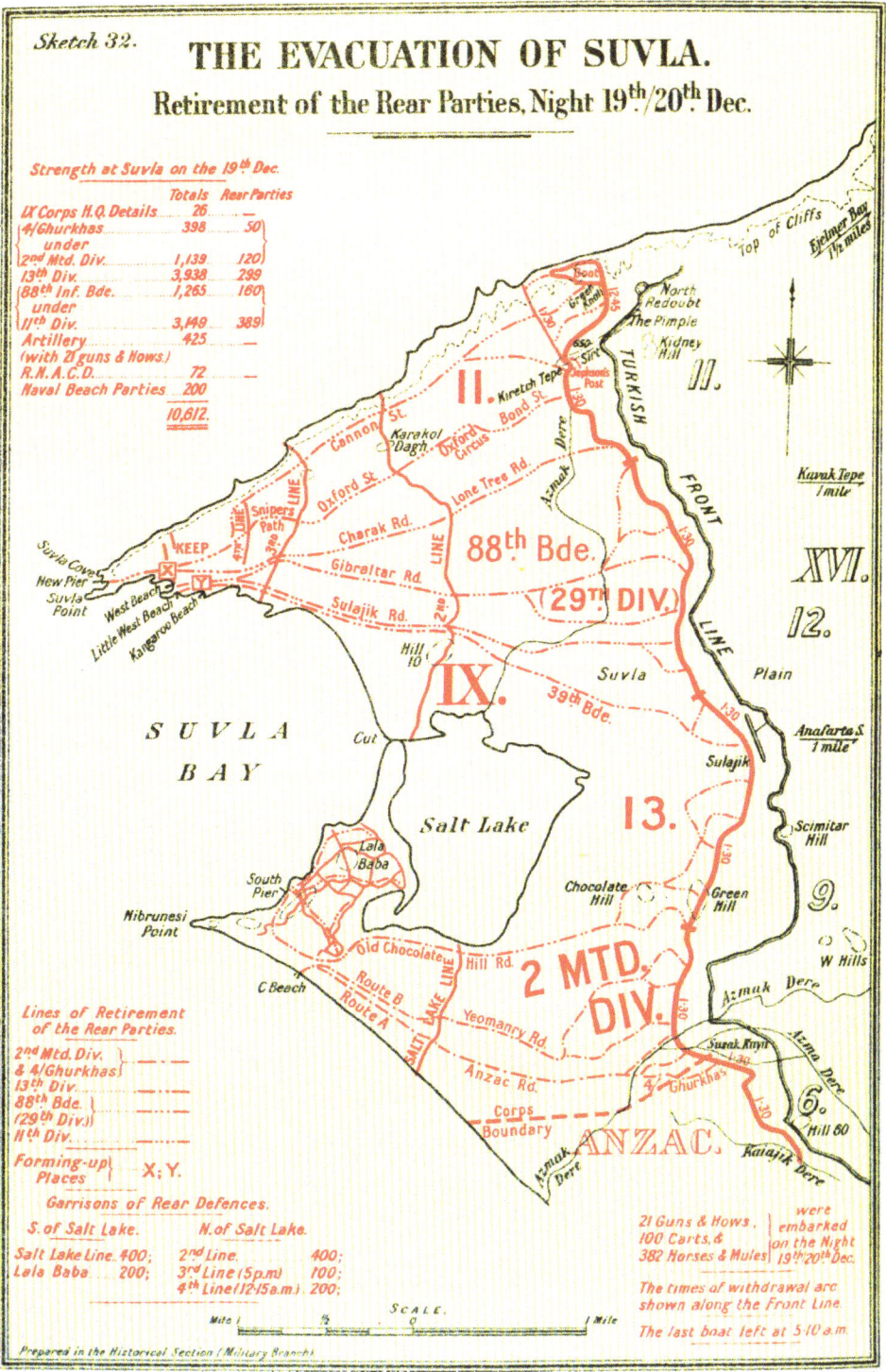

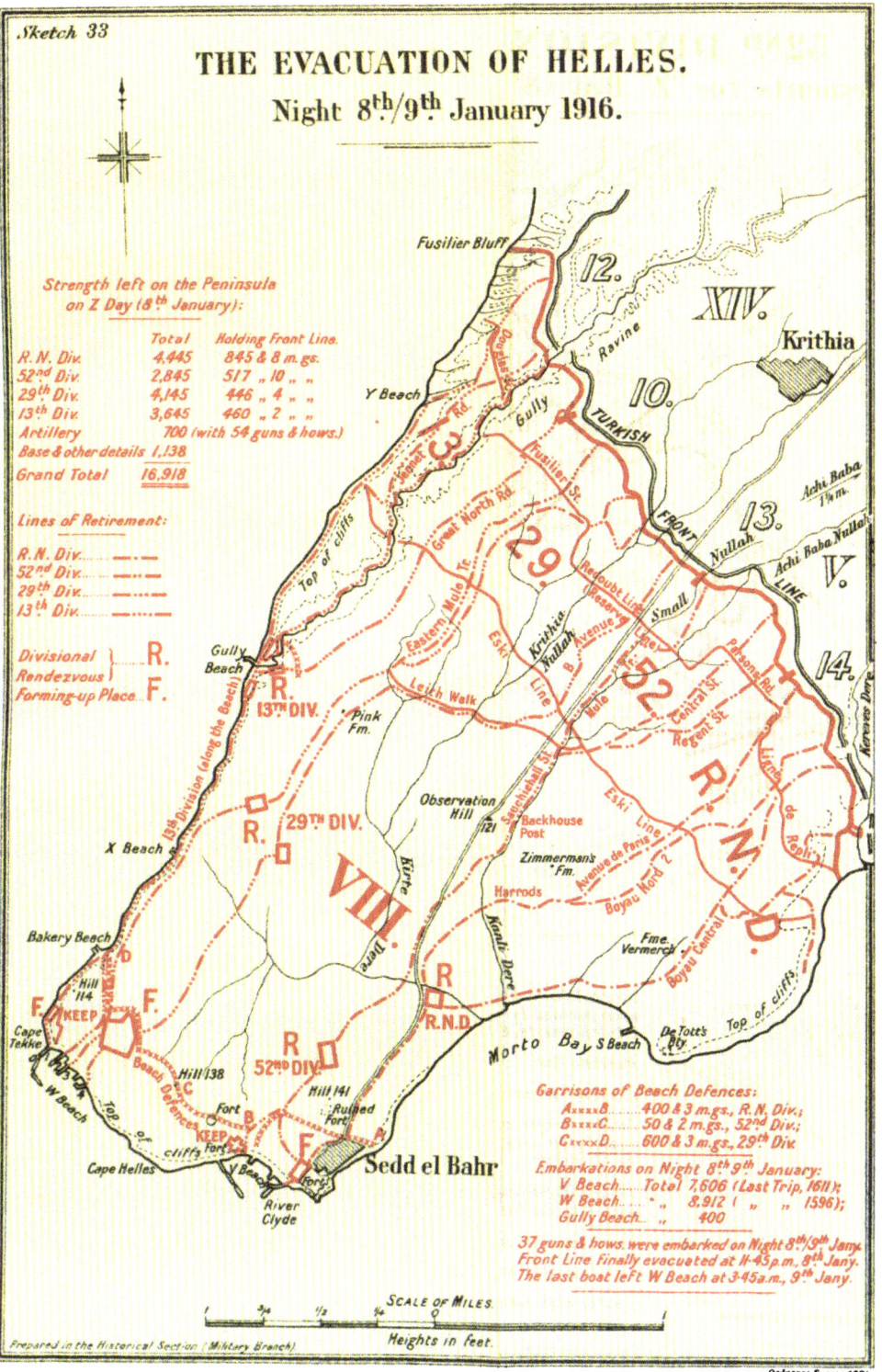

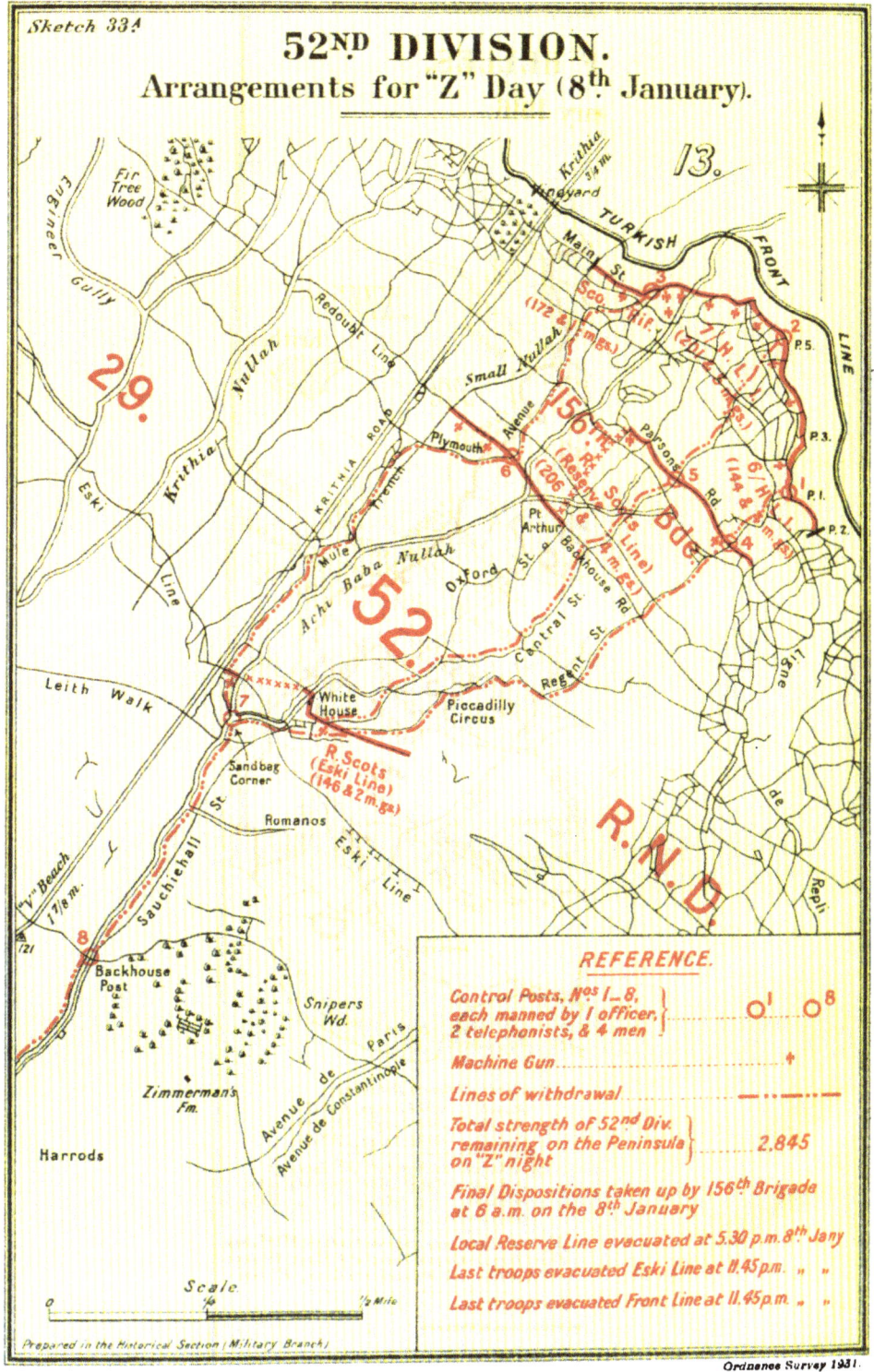

www.ingramcontent.com/pod-product-compliance
Lightning Source LLC
Chambersburg PA
CBHW040302170426
43193CB00021B/2977